A JOURNEY
FROM THE CHAIN BRIDGE
TO THE GOLDEN GATE

My parents, Sárika and Zoltán Biró, 1925

A JOURNEY
FROM
THE CHAIN BRIDGE
TO
THE GOLDEN GATE

BY

AGNES BIRÓ ROTHBLATT

SMALL
BATCH
BOOKS

Private Publishing of Personal Histories

493 South Pleasant Street
Amherst, Massachusetts 01002
413.230.3943
SMALLBATCHBOOKS.COM

*To Dan, Andre, and Steven Raul,
our wonderful sons,
and their families.*

CONTENTS

Introduction

Memories are like soap bubbles. They float by your mind's eye, they dazzle you for a moment, then puff, float away and disappear. Now that I am well into my seventies, I have decided to capture some of my memories and put them on paper, to preserve them before they float into oblivion.

This book is a collection of my childhood stories, memories of the second World War, stories of our escape from Hungary, arrival in the United States, assimilation to the new world, and living happily ever after—all in a compact book.

This is a coming-of-age story that I hope to share with the next generation and the one following, the grandchildren we are so proud of. They are mine, ours, yours, and everybody's. They will follow in our footsteps and pass on our traditions to their offspring, maybe in an updated "e version."

Some of my recollections are seen through rose-colored glasses. The facts about the family are as accurate as my limited knowledge permits me to recall. Since I have become the matriarch of the Biró family, I have no opportunity to compare notes or fact-check them with my peers. Some stories toward the latter part of the book have been inspired by my writing classes, where new ideas and topics were introduced. I found that my memories provided the inspiration here as well. They were etched very deeply in my mind.

Our family name is Biró. My given name is Ági, Agnes in America.

Sárika was my mom, Anyu in Hungarian, but I added a syllable and called her Nyunyu. Later, when she came to

1

America, she became Charlotte.

My dad was named Zoltán, shortened to Zoli, but whom I called Apu as a child.

Panni was my sister, Ann or Anna in the United States, who died much too soon.

Móricz (Morris) Szlovák was my maternal grandfather, called Nagypapa when we were growing up. He lived with us during and after World War II.

Aranka Szlovák was my maternal grandmother, called Nagymama, who died of a heart attack in her early sixties.

Andy and Sylvia Slovak were our uncle and aunt, who adopted my sister and me in the United States. Andy, or Andor, was my mother's older brother. Her eldest brother, Béla, died after trying to cross the Austrian border.

Rudi (Spitzer) Somogyi was a cousin of my grandfather, one of the relatives who survived the war.

The Oblaths include my paternal aunts, uncles, and cousins. My cousins Laci and Gyuri (Leslie and George) settled in London after they fled Hungary in the 1940s. Jozsef perished in a forced labor brigade in Germany in 1944.

The rest of the characters in my story are easily sorted out. They include Roger, who was my sister's wonderful husband, and Shike, who is my spouse and the father of our three fine sons.

Sári's Cookbook

The year was 1930. Sári received a thick, leather-bound, blank book with gold-embossed lettering on the cover. "My Favorite Recipes," it said. It was Sári's fifth wedding anniversary. She was a young bride trying to cook delicious dinners for Zoltán, her bank teller husband, who came home every day at noon from the local bank for his dinner.

She went to the other part of the house, where her parents lived. Mama and Papa, as she called them, lived in the adjacent apartment. You just had to cross the kitchen and you were in their sitting room. Mama was crocheting a round table cloth made up of rosettes. Mama made over a hundred snowflake design rosettes and stitched them together skillfully. They formed a perfect round when she finished.

"Mamika, what should we prepare today? We have some *lecso* and potato dumplings with apricot stuffing left from yesterday but Zoli likes a freshly cooked meal each day."

"Sárika, why don't you make *crepes-palacsinta* today and fill it with ground walnut paste. We can also make some with strawberry jam and cover it with vanilla sauce."

"Zoli will be sure to like that. He has such a sweet tooth."

Sárika thought these items should be recorded in her new cookbook. She entered: "Everyday Meals," "Easy to Fix." Her mother gave her the ingredients, all from memory. She went to the kitchen, where Marika, the maid, was washing the breakfast dishes.

"Marika, please go down to the market and get a dozen eggs, some milk, some powdered sugar, and we need fresh bread too.

3

We are making crepes for noon today. We have the jam, the walnuts in the pantry. See if there are any fresh vegetables available at the corner store. There should be some fresh peas or maybe some young kohlrabi that we could sauté with butter and parsley today."

Sárika went back to her cookbook and entered another chapter heading, "Spring Vegetables for Daily Vitamin Intake." She recorded her mother's procedure for cooking young peas, *borsofozelek*, and kohlrabi in the French style. Her mother had also instructed her how to make roux, or thickening, for the sauces. Soon she was getting ready to fix the meal by putting out all the utensils.

As the months went by, the cookbook started to fill up with new ideas for a variety of meals. When her friends came over for afternoon tea they chatted about new ways to prepare Sunday meals. Rózsika, her friend from Buda (one side of Budapest), knew of some new spices used in soups, tarragon and rosemary, that added a subtle flavor. Erzsi, another friend, had heard of a flourless cake made only with ground hazelnuts and butter, mixed with fine powdered sugar. Sárika would make notes and later entered the new ideas in her neat handwriting in the cookbook.

The years passed. In 1932 Sárika's first baby was born, Ági. Sárika learned how to prepare baby food: strained, grated carrots; finely pureed potatoes. As the baby grew she made homemade zwieback, or twice-baked toast, to help her teething. There was no ready-made baby food in Budapest back then.

In 1935 Sárika enrolled in a cooking course. She learned about sauces, soufflés, and roulades. She became the most popular hostess among her friends. She was considered "Sárika, the Super Chef." Her parties were celebrated. Her friends sent her bouquets of flowers and bottles of champagne before a soirée. Her husband Zoltán was moving up from his position as bank teller to head cashier at the bank. In the kitchen, the cook was scrubbing the vegetables and mixing the cake batter. The other maid, Marika, was moved to chambermaid position. She was even given a neat black dress with a white apron to wear when company came. The family acquired a new set of silver, place settings of flatware, four candelabras, and a silver compote fruit server. The coffee was served in demitasse cups with cobalt blue and gold rims on a silver tray.

Then, in 1939, Mama, Sárika's mother, suffered a heart attack. She was sitting with her two granddaughters, Ági, and Panni, born in 1936. She was teaching the little girls how to crochet when she fell ill. It seemed like a bad stomach flu at first but the doctor, Dr. Rosner, suspected it was more serious—her heart was beating irregularly. She was ordered to stay in bed and Dr. Rosner came over every day to check her pulse and to listen to her lungs with his stethoscope. She developed pneumonia, and oxygen tanks were delivered to help her breathe. A tent was made out of bedding to help her inhale peppermint vapors heated in a big pan of hot water and delivered to her bedside by Marika's strong arms. But she was not getting better. A few months later, Mamika died at home with her family at her bedside. Just before she passed away, in the final hours, the two grandchildren, Ági and Panni, were taken away to spare the young girls the sight of their grandmother's last struggle and death.

When Ági, who was about eight at the time, returned home the family—her parents, grandfather, and uncle—were sitting *shiva,* the customary mourning tradition of Jewish families. The adults sat on a low bench, said prayers for the dead, and received the condolences of friends, who dropped in and brought sweets. The mirrors were covered with black cloth. Everyone wore black mourning clothes. Nobody adorned his or her body. Regular dresses were taken to the cleaners and died black for this sad period. Even the jewelry was made of black stones.

In 1942, the war that engulfed Europe came to Budapest. Air raids became more frequent and the family made many trips to the air-raid shelter in the basement. The sirens wailed day and night.

The Biró family had an air-raid kit prepared by each bedside: a warm sweater, flashlights, a bottle of water, some dried nuts and fruits in case one had to stay downstairs for several hours, a book to read, some bandages, and aspirins. Food supplies became scarce. Margarine and lard became substitutes for butter, and meatless dishes were common. Noodles with jam and/or cottage cheese were eaten after watery ersatz soups.

Sárika started a new chapter in her cookbook, "*Haborus etelek*," or "Wartime Meals." She recorded the soups made out of beef bones and dried peas or beans. Dried grains were easy to store and did not need refrigeration. Big sacks of it were now filling the pantry, along with walnuts in their shells, flour from the country, and lard in pots, well covered so contact with air would not start spoiling them. Some smoked ham shanks were wrapped in old rags as well.

In 1944 the German troops occupied Hungary. Zoltán's job was terminated in the bank. No Jews were allowed in responsible positions. He was forced to join a labor brigade, a troop of men bound for military duty who were housed in barracks outside the city. They were used to clear away the debris and unexploded bombs that pelted and destroyed the factories and many residences in the city. Panni, Sárika, Grandfather, and Ági sewed on yellow stars to mark them as Jews. They had to leave their own comfortable apartment and moved in with another family in a ghetto house designated for Jews.

Sárika took her cookbook along. It became her diary and was her journal. The changes in lifestyle, cooking methods, and family events were all in there. Memories of her mother, Mama, her life as an aspiring socialite, her attempts as a creative cook, caring mother, and, later, survivor of a war-torn city, were recorded on those pages. The book's cover was no longer shiny but worn and faded. A decade and a half had gone by. It comforted her to look back at the past as the chapters reflected it. She covered the book with a clean newspaper and tucked it into her air-raid shelter pack. Maybe it would be useful after the war is over, she thought, or her two daughters might read it when the world normalized again.

Sárika was always an optimist about the future, and it kept her strong and forward looking.

In 1945 they emerged from the cellar. The siege of Budapest was over. The Russian troops liberated the city from the Nazi oppressors. The Biró family survived and was free to start a new life.

Zoli became too weak to work in the camp during that winter, due to the starvation diet he and his group were given. Luckily Zoli succeeded in escaping from the forced labor brigade with the help of a young guard whom Zoli rewarded with a gold coin sewn into his coat's lining. Zoli came home ill, with a hacking cough that would not stop.

Grandfather became quite frail. The two little girls, Ági and Panni, now ages thirteen and nine, were malnourished, tall, gawky, all skin and bones. Sári was the strong leader of the group. Their apartment was demolished in the bomb attacks. Only Zoli was able to climb up through the rubble and salvage some of their belongings.

Sári had a brilliant idea! She thought of purchasing the apartment on the fourth floor of the adjacent building. Two old bachelors lived there. Sári and Zoli approached them and an exchange deal was made with the help of some old golden jewelry. The family could move in shortly. The Birós had a roof over their heads again. The janitor helped them find some strong men to move the remaining beds, chairs, and tables to the new apartment.

The central heating was not functioning. It was damaged in the bombings so there was no heat in the apartment. The family huddled around a little makeshift "chestnut roaster," a small, round stove purchased from a neighbor. The smoke was vented through the window. The food now was survival fare—pancakes made with cooked dried peas and grilled on top of the stove. Snow had to be melted for drinking water. The pipes were all frozen, and the central water delivery system was not operating. There were no wells in Budapest, at least not in the area where the Birós lived. The Danube was badly polluted from all the debris and sewage dumped into it.

Sárika and Panni used to go foraging for pieces of wood, broken pieces of furniture to burn in the makeshift kitchen stove. Occasionally, they found an onion or a potato left behind in the warehouses along the Danube banks.

It was a miserable year, 1945, a bitter cold winter and chaotic recovery from all the deprivations caused by the siege of the city. There was not enough food, no access to laundry or bathing facilities, marginal cooking access, and the chestnut-baking stove smoked and broke down.

In September, however, the schools reopened and Ági and Panni returned to their classes. Many of their classmates were missing. Many were killed and some fled to the West with their families. As time went by, Sárika thought of teaching her daughters the skills every housewife knew—how to make easy meals with simple ingredients. Out came her magic cookbook. Recipes her mother had recorded were copied, so as not to put greasy fingerprints on her cookbook's pages. Panni learned to make soups. Ági was shown how to bake bread from raised flour dough. She loved to knead it and later watch the dough rise as it leavened. Later she added walnuts and raisins and turned it into *challah,* a holiday bread twist. Sometimes she added finely chopped onions or chives and more salt to the dough. Her innovations were entered into the cookbook.

Grandfather returned to services at the synagogue and Zoltán was reinstated at the bank. His health improved and he got a promotion. He was branch manager now. His office was at the end of the street, and he started coming home again for his noonday meals, as in the old days.

These were years of recovery and rebuilding for the Biró family, 1946, 1947, and 1948. But there were some black clouds gathering on the political horizon.

A First Memory

Here I am in my crocheted dirndl dress and my strong brown hiking shoes. Perched on my brown braids is a felt mountaineer's cap. I am hiking up the Matra Mountains with my father. I call him Apuka, Daddy in Hungarian. He wears a city suit, a shirt, and tie. He smokes a cigarette while we walk.

We took a train to this resort town in the mountains because I have the whooping cough. The fresh air will clear my bronchial passages and I won't "whoop" so much.

Apuka is not used to caring for me. Usually he is sitting at his desk at the office and he is busy writing.

My mother is in the hospital right now giving birth to my sister. She could not come on this trip. She is not strong enough to travel yet.

But Apuka and I get along very nicely. He asks me, "Do you want to pick some wild flowers, Ági? We could take them back to the hotel and put them on the table in a little vase. Everybody would enjoy them there."

I answer, "Yes, Apuka. I see so many blue and white flowers here. They all smell so fresh. I like flowers. They look like a lace curtain or like little bells."

I hurry along the path and am soon gathering a lovely bouquet. Then I trip and skin my knee. I get up and dust off my shoes. I pick some prickly weeds. They scratch my hands. They bleed. I cry. He puts his handkerchief around my bleeding fingers. He wipes my tears. He gives me a little kiss to make it better. We go back to the hotel and get dressed for dinner. I feel like a big girl. I am three years old.

Fun-Time in Winter

We live in Budapest, near the Danube, and close to our apartment house the tennis courts are covered with man-made ice, slick and smooth. We children can learn to skate. Panni is five, I am nine, and our mother, Nyunyu, bundles us in warm corduroy pants and cotton-lined jackets. We go to the skating rink together. We also sport hand-knit caps and gloves to keep warm. Our grandma crocheted them for such an occasion.

Winter in Budapest brings snow and ice on the Danube. It's cold. Jolly music is playing at Play-Land. Wiener waltzes, polka, *hop sa sa* blast from the loud speakers. The man at the ticket booth gives us the tickets for skate rentals. We sit on a long bench, and Nyunyu helps to fasten the skates onto our high-laced shoes. She uses a skate key to tighten the aluminum skates on. We get up. We wobble to the ice. The class for beginners is starting. There are four girls lined up along the railing: Susie, Eva, Mari, and Judit, our skate mates.

"One, two, glide and lift. Slowly. Hold on to the railing. One, two, lift, glide," says the instructor. He has a whistle around his neck. If we go too fast he blows it.

"Stay with the group, young lady." Eva has just slipped and falls on her rear. We hold on to each other and to the railing but we are slow in making progress. Learning to balance and move along is difficult

It is getting dark. We skate along. We'll come back tomorrow. Our mom is waving from the benches.

"Save some energy for tomorrow! Rome, too, was not built in a day. You did very well for a beginning."

She helps to take our skates off. We walk home, all tired out. We get hot cocoa when we return home, served in the nice china cups. It feels so good to be in our warm and cozy apartment. Our faces are red from the cold. But there is also a warm glow in our hearts. We tried something new and exciting. Soon we will glide on the ice and maybe even waltz along, thinking out loud with the optimism of the young at heart.

The Bridge

We were playing with our dolls, dressing them in party clothes for a tea party. The doll table was set with miniature china, cups and plates. My friend Panni (same name as my sister) and I were pretending to be little mothers. Just then my mother called, "Girls! It's time to wash your hands and come for lunch. Hurry up! Soup is on!"

The date was 1944. The place, Budapest, in our comfortable flat that faced the river Danube. We lived between the Parliament Building and the Margaret Bridge. You could see upstream from our windows. The bridge was a span from the Pest side of the city to the leafy, green Buda side. It also approached Margaret Island, which was a park-like setting for outings and sported a thermal bath for swimming, a frequently visited place in the summer months. We left our dolls and, as obedient girls, filed into the bathroom to get ready.

Then an enormous explosion deafened our ears. It seemed as if the house were shaking and moving. A long rumbling sound followed. "The world is coming to an end," I thought. Then the clatter of metal and more tumbling and scraping sounds. Dust clouds came in through the open windows.

Somebody was shrieking outside. The Margaret Bridge had exploded. Somebody had blown up the bridge. The people in the streetcars crossing the bridge were in the river. The entire bridge had collapsed. It was noisy and dusty. We could hear people calling for help. Bedlam and chaos ensued as rescuers attempted to approach the victims. Fire engines wailed and sirens blared emergency warnings. We huddled together in the back room seeking shelter and quiet away from the tragedy just outside our windows. We were taken by surprise, helpless and scared.

We were young children and had not experienced war so close by. Now, sixty-some years later, my friend Panni and I still relive those moments of surprise, shock, and anguish. We never played with our dolls after that. It seemed too childish, all at once.

The Yellow Star on Our Coats

The date was April 5, 1944. German troops had occupied Budapest two weeks earlier, on March 19, and Jews all over the city were staying close to their homes, cowering in their apartments, fearful of the occupying troops. Each day there was a new set of rules that restricted our lives and reduced our freedoms. On April 5 we could not go out into the streets without wearing a yellow star. The yellow star had to be canary yellow, 10 cm. in diameter, and firmly sewn onto our garments, right above our hearts.

I was a twelve-year-old girl and I was proud to be a Jew. I did not mind being identified as an "Israelite," the Hungarian term for being Jewish. I felt, in my youthful enthusiasm, that not only would they—our enemies—be able to tell who we were, but we would also know who our sisters and brothers were. So I wore my Star of David with pride and dignity. I announced to the world that I was a daughter of the covenant. I had my identity embossed inside and outside. It became a matter of the heart for me, and remains so to this day.

After April 5, 1944, many terrible things befell us: we were forced to move into a designated Jewish ghetto house; then my family and I went into hiding, using Christian papers, to spend much time in a bomb shelter; we suffered bombing and hunger; but our spirit never wavered. *Sh'ma Yisroel, Adonai Elohenu,* our Jewish God is One.

My First Day in a New School

"I have ironed your new uniform," my mother said softly. "It's hanging in your closet."

There it was, all starched and pressed: a striped blouse with a navy blue collar and a navy blue pleated skirt. I was nervous about my first day in the new school. It was where Jewish girls had to go, no longer to the public school where I had been going for four years. The Nazi restrictions forbade Jews to study with Catholics and Protestants. We were not permitted to attend the schools run by the state but had to crowd into the only existing Jewish day school in Budapest. It was 1944, and the restrictions on our freedom increased daily. We could not ride the streetcars, go to the movie theaters, or swim at the local sports center. We were second-class citizens. I felt sad, isolated, and ostracized, but curious too about the new school.

I got up early on Monday morning, a sunny, bright September day. I straightened my uniform so it fit just right, polished my brown shoes, and put a new beret over my long braids.

"I am leaving," I said and kissed my mother goodbye. My dad had been away for weeks, in a labor brigade clearing debris in a nearby town. Jewish men were not included in the military, even my dad who was a decorated veteran of the previous World War. He was now a common laborer doing community service, backbreaking work for a fifty-year-old man.

I reached the school building easily. It was not far from where we lived. I skipped up to the second floor and asked the teacher at the head of the stairs where Gymnasium I/a was. She directed me to a classroom to the right. About two-dozen girls sat on wooden benches with notebooks and pencils poised for the lesson to start. I discovered two girls that I knew from my old grade school, Panni and Zsuzsi. They were smiling and waving to me. I felt this was a good sign: I had friends nearby. After the bell rang, our teacher, Rózsinéni, entered. She was plainly dressed and had a short hairdo. She was around forty-five years old.

"I will talk seriously to you," she started. "You have to take your studies to heart because we are being watched. The police are keeping an eye on the comings and goings of all who are enrolled here. You must not attract attention or behave in a loud or boisterous way. You must leave quietly, not loiter outside, but return straight to your homes. You should not congregate in groups. Your schoolwork must be accurate, your papers handed in on time. You must share textbooks because there are not enough to go around. Today we will start with European history in the twentieth century."

The lesson was interesting, full of the lives of kings and queens, power struggles, wars, and assassinations. She showed us maps of how countries engulfed others and borders shifted. I was transfixed by all the detail that was presented.

Our second class was religious instruction. Our teacher was a young rabbi. The class was preparing for *Shabbat* services. The school decided that the new students would conduct the Saturday morning services. We sang the liturgy. We practiced reading the Hebrew prayers. At first we mumbled and bumbled over the Hebrew letters. Later we learned the blessings by heart. In a few months the class sang the *Sh'ma* in unison and recited the blessings fluently.

The weeks and the months went by rapidly. I became friends with most of the girls in my class. We loved our Hebrew teacher and often gossiped about him. One of the girls saw him in a coffee shop with his wife. He had a private life, to our amazement.

But as winter turned to spring our lives became more precarious. In April we had to sew on yellow stars that marked our Jewishness, and we faced ridicule, taunts, and catcalls from passersby on the street. We did not linger after school but hurried home to safety. Soon after that the school closed because Jewish girls were not allowed to attend school at all. Period. We were herded into ghetto houses and could only leave between 9 a.m. and 2 p.m.; otherwise, we were crowded into the one room assigned per family. My classmates and I became afraid for our lives. The iron fist of the Nazi regime crushed the last remnants of our free spirit. We became the victims of the Holocaust, most of us never to survive, and those lucky enough to live through it compelled to tell the story.

Going Into Hiding

The year is now 2004, and I am thinking of taking my twelve-year-old granddaughter to visit my native city, Budapest, Hungary. My mind goes back in time to when I was twelve, in 1944. Germany occupied Hungary and decided to kill all the Jews in Hungary along with all the Jews of Eastern Europe.

I am recalling the day when my sister and I went into hiding. We had already left the ghetto for a brief period earlier that year, when Raoul Wallenberg had given my family Swedish exemption papers so that we could live in a "safe house." But on October 15, 1944, Szálasi and the Hungarian Arrow Cross—the Hungarian populist Nazi party—started the regular and systematic elimination of the remaining Jews with nightly raids in the fifth district, along the river Danube. They took groups of defenseless women and children out to the banks of the river and shot them in a row until they fell into the turbulent cold water and died instantly.

It was time to save our lives, to flee, to hide. We, my sister and I, had Christian papers hidden in the bottom of the drawers. Our mother had purchased them from the caretaker that year for many ounces of gold. I was called Susan and my sister was called Judith, both real, live Catholic teenagers who grew up in the villages near Lake Balaton, far from Budapest. Our uncle took us by streetcar to the hiding place. It was in an abandoned apartment in the Zugló district outside the city. The prior residents had fled to the West and had left the key with a neighbor, my father's trusted friend, Géza. On the streetcar we tried to look as inconspicuous as possible. My hair

19

had been braided into tight knots with a big white bow. We wore two sets of clothes under loose-fitting jackets. My sister carried her doll. No packets. No rucksacks to make us look like refugees. We were just casual travelers going from the inner city to the suburbs.

At the end of the 49 line we got off and walked to Kassai ut, our destination. The streets were all dark. The houses were prepared for air raids. Dark sheets covered all the windows. We stumbled in the dark until we found number 3/a, a two-story apartment building. The key was given to our uncle by Géza and he quietly let us in. Shattered glass was everywhere. The next building had been hit in an air raid and the windows in our new home were all blown out. We could not turn on the light so we groped around with the help of a flashlight. We saw blood drops and bloody finger prints everywhere. The shattered glass had cut the previous residents as they tried to clean up. We found a broom in a closet and cleared our way. We found some pillows and blankets in the closet. We made makeshift beds on the couch. We went to the kitchen and made some tea on the stove. We spoke in whispers, scared by the eerie discomfort of the place. This was our first night away from our parents and away from the shelter of our old home. We huddled together and hardly spoke. Our teeth chattered from the cold.

I don't recall anything else from that day. We probably fell asleep. Our mother was able to join us the next day. She took our grandfather by the hand, and they went unnoticed on the same streetcar route that we had taken.

The Coal Cellar

We had been in the cellar for two weeks. It was the coal cellar of a small apartment house on the outskirts of Budapest. Back then, in the 1940s, each apartment had its own bin in the basement where a winter's supply of coal was kept to be used for the furnace as needed. It had been a cold, bitter winter and by now, in December, much of the mound of the black, dusty chunks had been flattened and we could make our beds on top of it. We used rugs to pad it, then layers of blankets and pillows. We had to snuggle together, my sister, mother, and I, to stay warm and to feel safe. We wore warm stockings, long dresses, and bulky sweaters because it was so cold, as well as damp, in the cellar. We were chilled to the bone and our uncovered skin was black from the coal dust.

We had been hiding in this underground shelter from the frequent bomb attacks on the city. The Second World War was in its final, furious phase. The Russian troops were just miles outside the city and the Germans were still ravaging the populace. The air artillery was continuous, trying to shoot down Allied planes. Bombs whizzed and exploded day and night, and there was nowhere to hide. We lived with nightmares by day as well as night. One of the worst parts was when we heard walls crashing after an explosion. We were unable to tell what was happening to the house above us, where my father was hiding.

My mother and we girls had been living in that apartment for months, incognito, with false documents verifying our assumed identities. My father had snuck in later, having escaped from a forced labor brigade that defused unexploded bombs. He had fled when the guards were not watching and walked the many miles to our hiding place, hiding during the day and moving only at night, hidden by the total blackout. Then, one night, we heard the pre-arranged code knock at the door, the familiar first few bars of Beethoven's fifth symphony, reassuring us that it was him! He fell into my mother's arms. He was emaciated, tattered, and cold, his shoes in shreds, but deliriously happy to be with his family. Since then he lay recovering in a corner daybed, still hiding, now from the other apartment house dwellers. Then came the air attacks. While we could flee to the relative protection of the coal cellar, he could not. He had to remain in the line of fire, helpless and alone.

In the cellar we sat on top of the coal bin loudly saying prayers, "Our Father who art in heaven, hallowed be thy name…," while in our minds we cried, *"Sh'ma Yisroel, Adonai Elohenu…."* We were Jewish, mimicking our Christian neighbors with Catholic prayers. It was dark in the cellar, our only lights flickering candles. Electricity was long gone; the power plants had been bombed first. I hear my mother snoring, exhausted from the struggle for survival, while my sister, to cover our mother's noisy breathing, said even more loudly, "Our Father who art in…."

At last the bombing and shooting stopped, followed by long silence. Hours went by with no air activity! What was happening?! The cellar remained quiet as its residents dozed off, we included, for the night. In the morning, loud knocking and voices woke us.

"Open up! Hand over your weapons! We are Russian liberating troops! We have defeated the German forces and have liberated your city! We will not harm you! We are your friends!"

A new era had dawned. We learned to speak a new language, *"Govarit PaRuskis"* was the mode, but we were all equals again.

Remembrance of Summers Past
Badacsony, c. 1943

It is a warm, muggy afternoon. The flies are buzzing around us on the veranda. It is a long enclosed porch in front of our country house in the vineyard. We are sitting at the rattan dining set, in the middle of the enclosure. To the far left, Grandfather is taking a snooze. To the far right, Nyunyu, our mother, is planning the next day's meals with Rózsika, our cook.

"We will need carrots, parsnips, onions, garlic, and saffron for the chicken soup."

Mrs. Virág brought a nice plump hen for the pot.

"Then we'll make apple strudel for dessert. Please peel about ten of the green apples we have in the pantry and slice them thin. We have raisins and cinnamon. The strudel dough should be stretched in the morning."

I am with my sister, Panni, and our friend Panni, who is visiting us from Budapest. Our thoughts are on a hide-and-seek game we are planning.

My sister Panni, seven years old, is a slender, blonde-haired girl who loves plants, flowers, and animals. She looks after the caretaker's dog with table scraps plentifully taken over daily. She plays with her dolls, tucks them in, and talks to them. She is a sweet and gentle girl. Friend Panni, who is eleven years old, has gone to school with me since grade one. We talk to each other for hours as we walk home from school. She and her family live across the street from us on the Danube Quay, at Klotild utca in Budapest. Panni is smart and knows the facts of life better than I do. She has an older brother who informs her.

She wears glasses and is a good student. We look at each other and think of something to do.

I am Ági, also eleven years old, and I have long brown braids. I am robustly built, not chubby, but big boned. I think of myself as the big sister, the ring leader of my small group. I usually have a glint in my eye.

Nyunyu, our mother, is the captain of the ship. She guides and directs this household with expertise and skill. Our father, Apu, is in the city. He commutes to the vineyard by train on weekends. He has an important job at the bank and he is not to be disturbed with household problems. Grandfather is the man in charge of running the estate. He hires and fires the agricultural workers who keep the vineyard thriving. He schedules the caretaker in his daily tasks. There are two horses, one cow, one pig, and a flock of chickens that Mr. Kovacs and his wife look after.

So back to the veranda, where we sit and we feel bored and ready for some adventure.

"We will hide in the wine cellar and nobody will find us. We will go behind the barrels where it is dark and spooky. The cobwebs will cover us and we will be invisible."

We tiptoe out of the house and we think nobody even notices us. Grandfather is still snoring. Nyunyu goes to the kitchen to see if the flour bin is full enough for the strudel dough. Our kitten, Cicu, follows us. We walk under the walnut trees, past the deep well into the peach orchard, and to the cellar. It looms before our eyes. Then we notice that Grandfather has put the big padlock on after he served some wine to the caretaker. Foiled in our plan, we pick some figs behind the cellar. The sweet nectar runs off our fingers. Then a bee comes and stings my palm. I run home crying, wanting to be consoled by our loving mother. She dips my hand in vinegar to take out the sting. She bandages me and I am ready for a game of cards. All in a lazy summer afternoon.

The next day the group goes for a swim at Lake Balaton. The caretaker brings the two horses and the buggy to the front of the house. My mother gets in first, then the two Pannis, Rózsika the cook, and myself. The lake is about an hour's ride through the cornfields, wheat, and rye, and cornflowers in neat rows. We reach the village, where Rózsika gets off and picks up two bottles of cold soda water at the general store and some pretzels for our midday snack. We soon arrive at the "strand"— the bathing beach with a neat row of wooden cabins in which we can change our clothes. We have pails, shovels for the sand, rubber tubing to float in, rattan mats to lie down on. Rózsika unfolds some lounge chairs to sit on. We are all set for a day in the sun and the cooling water of the lake. Nyunyu puts suntan lotion on our noses and on our shoulders. Freedom.

Who gets in the water first? We all run to get there.

A Remembrance of Things Past
April 15, 1944

Sárika woke up with a sudden shock. She closed her eyes again. No! This was a day she found hard to start. Her emotions started to take over and her spirit was full of rebellion. Why? Why, oh God, do we have to be singled out and suffer our neighbors' discrimination and jeers? What have we done to be marked like sheep getting readied for slaughter? Why do we have to wear a yellow star? But she, her family, and friends had already sewn the yellow stars on their clothes. The German occupying forces had decreed that all Jews are to be marked to make sure that they can be identified among the Hungarian population. She had sewn the stars on the left side of her jacket, on her husband Zoli's topcoat, on the two young girls' sweaters—as well as on her old father Móricz's overcoat. She dreaded going down to buy bread and milk. She wondered how people would treat her. Would they utter anti-Semitic remarks? Or would they ignore the yellow star?

She was going to meet her friend Klári today, although she was afraid to leave the house. Klári lived a fairly long streetcar ride away, in the industrial section of Budapest. Klári's husband, Felix, managed a box manufacturing plant and the Balzers lived on the plant grounds. The two women, Sári and Klári, planned a heart-to-heart talk. It had been only four weeks since the Germans occupied Hungary and the oppressive changes had been felt. People were picked up and taken to detention centers randomly. At night there were surprise knocks on the doors and men were taken to unknown locations and not heard from later.

26

Men of military age were told to report to forced labor camps and for hard labor. Life had become full of fear and uncertainty. In spite of her apprehensions, Sári rose, washed, and dressed in a cheerful flowered dress, combed her hair in a loose bun, and put a little rouge on her cheeks. She tried to present an attractive appearance.

Mariska, the cook, was already putting breakfast on the table: coffee, milk, some poppy seed cake, and jam. The girls will be up soon and have to get ready for school. Zoli, her husband, was no longer employed at the bank. He had to leave his position, in accordance with Jewish restrictions. He was packing his clothing to go to the registration center for the forced labor battalion. He was looking for his waterproof jacket in the hall closet, and was setting out the items that he needed to take along. Grandfather Móricz was getting dressed to go to morning prayers at the nearby synagogue.

The Biró family lived in Budapest, near the Danube, on the Pest side of the city. Their home was in a large apartment house on the fourth floor. They occupied five rooms for the family and the household help. The girls were looked after by Fraulie, a German governess who had lived with them for more than five years. Fraulie loved the girls, Ági and Panni, as if she were their grandmother. She dressed them, combed their long hair, practiced German with them, and walked them to school. According to the new restrictions, she would not be able to work for a Jewish family anymore. She would be forced to return to Germany at the end of the month. Leaving the family that she had grown to love and feel at home with saddened her heart. Fraulie had no more family in Germany, and she was too old to look for a new line of employment.

Later that day Sári decided to leave the security of her home and to step into the busy streets. She encountered the janitor by the elevator. Mr. Nagy greeted Sári warmly and they chatted about the weather.

"It's pretty windy today. Be sure you button your jacket, Mrs. Bíró. My wife baked some *pogácsa*. Come in later and let me give you a sample."

At the dairy store Aunt Rózi poured an extra deci of sour cream into Sári's milk jug "so that the children can have a good supper tonight." Milk, bread, butter were purchased with rationing coupons and the weekly allotment was too little to keep growing children well nourished. At the bakery a long line was queuing up. The bread shipment had arrived late. The bread was dark, coarse, and not fully baked. It was doughy, heavy, and chewy. Sári was happy that she got into the bakery while the supply lasted, and put her loaf in her basket quickly.

Next she went to the butcher shop and tried to stock up on lard and some sausage. She wanted to have some supplies for the hard time she expected yet to come. When she returned home she stopped in at the concierge's as planned. When she entered the concierge's apartment, a nice waft of cooking odors gave her a little cheer. Mrs. Nagy was sitting at the kitchen table and a cup was set out for Sári too. With the warm milk, black coffee, and sweet sugar cubes, Mrs. Nagy offered her *pogácsa*, a round muffin traditionally made from bacon bits and flour.

"We know how hard things are for you and your family now, Mrs. Bíró, since the Jewish laws have come to restrict your freedom and mobility. We hear from our friends that even worse days are ahead for you. There are concentration camps in Poland and Germany, and the Polish Jews have already been gathered in a camp outside of Krakow. You and your family must go into hiding and disappear. You should get some Christian papers and go to the countryside where nobody knows you. People are fleeing from the advancing Russian troops in Transylvania and you could pretend to be one of those families. If you find shelter in the western part of Hungary, say near Lake Balaton, you may escape these Nazi murders."

Sárika finished her coffee, wrapped the muffin in a paper

napkin, sighed deeply, thanked the Nagy couple, and went upstairs. Zoli had finished packing. Grandfather had said his morning prayers and was home again. The girls had left for school with Fraulie a while ago.

Sárika related to the two men in her life what she heard from Mr. and Mrs. Nagy a few minutes ago. "What should we do to survive this awful persecution? How can we save our family?"

Grandfather suggested that maybe the family could get Christian birth certificates from the caretakers in the vineyard. They had been employed by the Bírós for many decades and had demonstrated their trustworthiness and honesty. Zoli was thinking of his friends at the bank. Géza was a liberal and freedom-loving man. Maybe he would help find a hiding place. He would try and talk to him today. There was so much to do and so little time. Sári said goodbye to her beloved husband. He had to report to the Jewish labor battalion today. She hoped he would not be kept there yet. Her heart was heavy and her spirits were low. She decided to keep her appointment with Klári at her Lehel Street home. She bravely got on the yellow #4 streetcar that headed in that direction. Her friend Klári came to the door but she was not smiling when they embraced.

"Sárikám, welcome," she said. "*Isten hozott.* You are a strong woman to go out, take the streetcar, and go about your business today, the first day that we have to wear the yellow star. How did it go? Did anybody make a remark or taunt you on the streetcar? Did you feel scared? Was there an unpleasant incident?"

"No," answered Sári. "I am alright. *Minden rendben.* People treated me politely."

"I thank you for coming," said Klári. There is so much we have to talk about: our future, our family's safety, our survival. We, the women, have to make the plans to prevent the evil process that the Germans have designed, to kill us all for sure. Our husbands are engaged to service in the forced labor battalion. We have to slip out of the noose and escape before it is too late and all our freedoms have been regulated. We must act now."

Sári replied, "I have talked to Mr. and Mrs. Nagy, the janitors in our apartment house. They encouraged me to go into hiding with my girls. We may be able to get some Christian birth certificates from the caretakers in the vineyard. All this needs secrecy, lots of money, and carefully laid plans. I am going to write to the relatives of the caretakers and ask them to bring us some food from the country. When I see them in person, I will approach them about the papers. I also plan to sell my gold jewelry so that I have some available cash as needed for our escape. Zoli has a friend in the bank who may know of a hiding place for us in the outskirts of the city. We must pull things together in the next few weeks, before newer Jewish laws are declared."

Klári was smiling now. She related that she too was planning to disappear with her eight-year-old daughter to the country. She was going to take a job in a spa as an attendant in one of the resorts in the lake region. She had learned Swedish massage and hoped this skill could be utilized now. She decided to comb her hair differently and use makeup like her Christian neighbors use. Fortunately, neither Sári nor Klári had Semitic features, and they were young, slender women. They would try to pass as non-Jews.

The two women made a pact to attempt to outwit the Nazis and survive at all costs, and afterwards tell the world about their story. The life-affirming game they were about to do should not go undocumented and forgotten. They were about to make history. As it was getting late, Sári said farewell to Klári. They parted with a warm hug and tears in their eyes.

"I hope we can keep in touch, but if not we'll meet after it's all over. *Isten veled*," said Sári, as she walked away with head held high.

Returning to the Old Home
January 30, 1945

We are back in Klotild utca, where I grew up, in our old home.

We had left home hurriedly on October 16 to go into hiding in Zugló when Szálasi and the Arrow Cross Nazis took over the final phase of the killing of the Jews in Hungary. We then spent three months in a one-room apartment at Kassai út 3/a. Méhes Geza, Apu's loyal friend, found this empty apartment for us. Its rightful owner was away somewhere on the Russian front. He trusted Geza with his keys, and with Geza's brave help we took shelter there. I was Zuzsa Kapetter, Panni was Judith Kapetter, and Nyunyu was Ilona Kapetter: the names on our Christian papers. We had "fled" Transylvania from the Russian troops. We also had Grandfather with us. His Christian papers called him Vendell bácsi, Uncle Vendell, an old pensioner from our village.

The days at Kassai út were scary. We huddled together silently and tried to keep warm. The windows were all broken after an air raid dropped a bomb nearby. At night, Uncle Geza came and taped the windows shut so that the wind would not whistle in and rain would be kept out. When the bomb attacks became constant, we had to go down to the coal cellar, the space below the house. The other residents slept on the same mattresses. There was Mrs. Kiss and her two kids, a boy about nine and a girl of four. At night Mrs. Kiss would wake Nyunyu up to complain that she was on Mrs. Kiss's side of the narrow mattress. There was also Aunt Therese, who was old and sick. Her feet were swollen and she could not walk. She used a cane and hopped around as best she could. Her feet were wrapped in rags to keep warm. She prayed constantly, reciting the rosary. We were supposed to pray along. It was dark, and the monotonous prayer soon put Nyunyu to sleep. To cover up the sound of her snoring we prayed louder and louder, trying to protect her. We went outside only for bathroom breaks and to gather snow, which we used for drinking water. The pipes were frozen and there was no running water. When it was quiet—no airplanes roaring—we would go upstairs, change clothes, and find some dry bread to eat. Nyunyu had wisely saved a large piece of smoked bacon, which would nourish us with the bread. The only other food that I remember were some red beets, which we had bought some weeks earlier, boiled and sliced up. It was so cold that we did not need a refrigerator. The beets were almost frozen in the dish where we left them.

After nights and nights in the coal cellar, one morning, on January 8, there was a knock on the door. It was a Russian soldier, then three more Russian soldiers with guns drawn.

"Open up! *Germaniski soldaten?*" they demanded.

We hugged them at first, then got scared because they were rude and demanding, wondering if we did not harbor German soldiers.

We cowered once more, afraid for our lives. We had to put our hands up. They searched us, for weapons? And the men found that their pocket watches were confiscated while being searched. Soon other soldiers came back, looking for *"blondines,"* blonde women. My mother smeared her face with coal and pulled her headscarf over her face to look old.

The next night two soldiers brought a bucket of vodka and asked everyone to drink along with them. Grandfather tried to act strong to protect the helpless women. My mother was forty years old at the time. Mrs. Kiss was even younger. Aunt Therese was in her seventies. I myself was twelve and my sister only eight years old. Well, the vodka inebriated the soldiers and we barely escaped with our lives. We locked ourselves into the coal storage compartment and they luckily didn't notice our absence. I only remember loud noises, Russian singing and scuffling. Then all was quiet. The vodka had run out and they left to look for more to drink.

We decided the next day to return to our old apartment, since it was in the center of the city and more protected than the suburban Kassai Street. Fortunately, the following day my two cousins, Laci and Gyuri Oblath, appeared at the door, two disheveled, ragged, unshaven characters. All they carried was a ham hock, wrapped in a rag.

"We were liberated in Csepel," said Laci.

The two had been in a forced labor battalion in Csepel, the industrial camp just below the city, an island where the Weiss Manfred factory made weapons and military supplies. Because of this they were heavily bombed by the Allies. The Nazis sent the still able-bodied Jewish boys and men to clear away the debris.

My father had been there as well and now he came straggling in shortly after his nephews, Laci and Gyuri, had arrived. My father had left Csepel with the help of one of his guards, whom he paid with a gold coin that had been sewn into his jacket. My father was afraid to make the trip alone, around three to four hours on foot, because the Germans, along with the Hungarian Arrow Cross, would still shoot Jews without any hesitation. So the soldier seeming to have a prisoner was really protecting my father on his journey to us.

My cousins and Apu told us that Budapest was burning, that houses were in ruins, and that corpses littered the roads where they fell. Some of the streets still had barricades where the Russians and the locals battled each other. They were not sure if the building where we once lived still stood. It was on the edge of the Danube, still a battleground from the Buda side. The two young men and my father decided to make the trip back to investigate the situation before we all went back. They left early and they got back late at night. On the way they bought a hand-pulled cart to pack up our meager belongings. The next day we looked for the handcart that had been pulled into the doorway by the stairs but it was gone. My mother was in tears.

"What will we do next? We cannot carry our ungainly bundles in our hands!"

We were weak from weeks of malnutrition and fear. My mother approached a friendly-looking Russian soldier and said, "The cart is stolen. I left it here last night. What are we to do?" The soldier patted her on the back.

"You wait here. I get you another one."

After a while he came back with a similar simple carrying cart that two people could pull along. The trip back to Klotild utca was long and tiresome. We chose to go by the main thoroughfares, by Heroes Square, Andrassy út, all the way to the bombed-out and smoldering *Nyugati pályaudvar* (train station to the West). Then we approached Klotild utca from the Berlini tér end.

Along the way the family's strength gave out. After Gyuri and Laci pulled the cart, my mother and father took turns. It was just too heavy. They were weak from hiding, starving, and being cold. My mother spotted a horse and buggy along Andrassy út. She bargained with the owner—how much would it be if he took us to our destination? The driver asked for a huge sum of money plus some food. My mother agreed and we repacked our stuff on his cart, tied the handcart to the wagon, and proceeded on our way. I remember that the horse was so emaciated that his ribs poked out of his wrinkled hide.

Slowly we made it to our old home. Just as we arrived, the Germans started to fire at us from across the Danube. They thought that we brought a cannon and ammunition, not just bundles of clothing and pots and pans. The horse was hit and died instantly. We barely escaped, hiding under the doorway.

The men in our family were quick to realize the dangers and shoved us into safety.

So, here we are, not in our old nice apartment but in an office on the first floor, where the mining company conducted its accounting business. The desks are along the walls. We put our suitcases on the floor and mother covered it with some rugs that she salvaged. With a few bags of dry and clean clothing we make pillows for ourselves. Luckily we brought back some woolen blankets to cover ourselves. There is no electricity, only a carbide lamp. It is a makeshift light made from some metal drums and a candlewick. It smells awful, but at least we can see. There is one water faucet down the hall where everybody lines up and fills containers with water. This is our life after the siege in January 1945.

Life After the Seige
March 30, 1945

The city is slowly coming back to life. People are venturing out from their hideaways. Bartering has become a way of getting food, especially near the railroad stations and the boulevards. The trains are only running in some places, and villagers crowd inside and on top of the trains, to bring potatoes, flour, carrots, and dried peas to the city. In exchange they take used shoes and dresses and bedding back home. Stores are still burnt out, but looting has stopped. There are Russian soldiers on street corners instead of police. Trucks zoom rapidly and carelessly along the boulevards, mostly military vehicles packed with Russian soldiers. There are no traffic lights and the trucks are a danger to pedestrians crossing the streets.

We get a sack full of dried peas, flour, and cooking oil. Nyunyu buys a chestnut-roasting stove, which we use to cook on and to heat our room. It is vented through the window. We cut a hole into a metal plate and placed it in one of the windowpanes. The smoke goes out to Klotild utca. Other people have made similar inventions to survive. (Necessity is the mother of all inventions.) We make pea pancakes, which are not good even on an empty stomach. They are gooey and bland.

We have a new member of our household, Weisz Jancsi, the son of Nyunyu's best friends, Erzsi and Miklos Weisz. Jancsi is an orphan now. Last December, in the final days of the Nazi occupation, his parents were taken out of their yellow-star ghetto house and shot into the Danube. We celebrated his sixteenth birthday on February 9, 1945, with the last of the bacon we

36

had saved. Jancsi's favorite activity is to look into the desks that the employees of the mining company have left behind. He has found packs of cigarettes and remnants of chocolate bars, which he sells or swaps with vendors and makes a profit.

We all stay close to our room at night because the Russian solders accost pedestrians and rob them of watches and other consumer goods. We are still scared for our lives. We feel so vulnerable in our makeshift house. When Russian soldiers enter the floor, people signal each other through the walls. Grandfather puts some paper in the fire to smoke out the intruders. People say now, jokingly, *"Biróék ujra kodositenek."* "The Biró family is once again putting up a smoke screen." It is not funny, but true.

Traveling Back to the Vineyard
July 7, 1945

We are back in Bács at the vineyard. We felt safe enough to get on the train at Délipalya udvar and take the slow Balaton-bound passenger train. The trains are running without disruption now that the tracks have been repaired but it took seven hours to arrive at Badacsony-tomaj.

Our compartment was jam packed with another family, a chubby young mother with two children carrying big bundles and suitcases. They were moving to the grandparents, who lived in Tapolca. The father had died on the Russian front. They were moving back to the old village where their grandparents lived because life in Budapest had gotten to be too difficult. Housing in Budapest was in short supply after bombs had ruined every third building. But at the grandparents' place in the old village there was a big house.

We had a delicious lunch packed for our trip to Bács. Nyunyu had found some hard rolls at the bakery and she had made bologna sandwiches and a thermos with sweet tea. Grandfather lives at the vineyard. He had cleared out the old country house of all the dirt and the belongings of the Hungarian military family who had been stationed there when the Jews in the village were expelled. Now we return to our second home.

Grandfather was waiting for us with a cart and horses. At the vineyard newly stuffed straw mattresses and whitewashed clean walls had been readied for our coming. Mr. and Mrs. Virág help grandfather get the work done. They had been our caretakers for twenty years. They live in a separate house at the bottom of the hill. They tend the livestock and plant and maintain a vegetable garden. Their daughter Rózsika used to be our nanny in Budapest. When the Nazis came to power she had to return home. The new law forbade Jews to have non-Jewish household help, so she could not stay with us. She was eighteen years old then and fell in love with the neighbors' son, Papp Geza. They married and now have a little boy, Józsi. They all live together. Rózsika, like her mother, is an excellent cook and makes delicious dinners for us. Yesterday we had *paprikás krumpli*, potatoes with roasted onions, fresh paprika, and some dry sausage that they still had in the pantry. It was aromatic and delicious, a perfect birthday treat for all of us. Yesterday I turned thirteen.

I am happy to be here where life seems to be quieter and less hostile than in the city. Panni and I sleep a lot. It is so quiet, only the flies are buzzing in the window. We feel at peace here.

Panni and I explore the garden and climb the fruit trees. The cherries have been picked but we still find some late-ripening clusters on the high branches. We pick them and eat them right away. We also helped pick peppers. I am enlisted to help with the potato peeling and we watch Mrs. Virág churn butter.

Little Józsi is so cute. He walks now and talks. He says some words he heard like: *boci,* papa, mama, *gyere, jó fiu* (calf, dad, mom, come, good boy). The little dog is his friend. Csöpi dog follows him around and they get into a lot of mischief.

I am amazed that the war, the bombs, and the deprivations did not affect the life of people in the countryside. There is normalcy, maybe simplicity, and a continuation of the old-fashioned country lifestyle, which can be observed and then embraced by our family who has been through so much.

These enclaves of self-sustained villages survived, and it was only later that they were swept along by the big brooms of the Russian-Hungarian Communist dictatorships of Josef Stalin and Mátyás Rákosi, the Hungarian prime minister.

Panni's Illness, 1947-1948

After about a year we were settled in to our new apartment at Klotild utca 3/a with what was left of our furniture.

Panni, Grandfather, and I moved to the courtyard side of the apartment. We had three couch-like beds along the walls. We liked sharing the room with Grandfather. But illness started to present itself in all of us. Nyunyu had frostbitten feet. She could only wear Apu's wider, men's shoes. Grandfather needed a chamber pot because he had to get up so often during the night to urinate. I developed hepatitis, with terrible stomachaches and with my eyes turning yellow. The remedy was a strict diet, no fat, only dry toast with dry cheese. I was so sick I had to rest every afternoon. It took me weeks of dieting and resting to feel better.

Then Panni had a high fever. Even aspirin and cold compresses did not help. Nyunyu called over Dr. Rosner, who lived across the street in Klotild út 4. He listened to Panni's heart, checked her lungs, throat, joints. After a very thorough examination, he shook his head with real concern. He diagnosed strep throat. Panni needed penicillin, but penicillin was not available in Hungary at that time. Nyunyu sent a telegram to our uncle and aunt, Andy and Sylvia, in Rockford, Illinois. I still remember how she phrased her plea:

"Pannika very sick. Please send penicillin soon."

Dr. Rosner gave Panni some injections to bring her fever down. She was not to get up from bed. Her heart was affected by the throat infection. She had rheumatic fever. Nyunyu made chicken soup and lemonade, all very scarce items on the black market.

Panni had little appetite and she had a hard time getting food down her throat. They brought her ice cream from a pastry shop, which she enjoyed.

After several days of anxious waiting, the penicillin arrived. I don't remember how, because the mail was not delivered yet internationally from the United States to Hungary. I think it came via an attaché of the American consular corps. The ampoules of penicillin were delivered to Dr. Rosner across the street, who would give Panni a shot every four hours. Even during his office hours he would come over in his white office coat and cheerfully tell Panni that it was time for another shot. The shots were painful because the medicine was diluted in an oily solution. Panni would wince and take it bravely.

Panni was bedridden for several months. At the end of her bed rest her muscles were all weak. She had to learn how to walk again, to retrain her muscles. When she was stronger, she had to go to the hospital to have her tonsils taken out. Nyunyu moved in at the hospital and stayed with her for three days. Now it was time for more ice cream because Panni's throat was so sore. She could not talk. So she wrote notes to Nyunyu. Nyunyu saved these love notes. Nyunyu got a bead-stringing kit to entertain Panni. Nyunyu made lovely bracelets and necklaces for her with the colorful beads, little flowers strung in rows. She also got Panni lots of books to read. One of her favorite books was Erich Kaestner's *Emil and the Detectives*. It was a book about a boy who was robbed taking a train to see his grandmother in a distant city. The money was pinned to his pocket and he recovered the money with the proof of the pinholes in the cash.

Panni was a skinny little girl when she got sick, and by the time she recovered she was a young adolescent. She put on weight and filled out. She was going on twelve. She needed new clothes and she got her hair cut in a stylish bob. Her eyes had a new sparkle. She was ready to rejoin her peers at school.

She was over her long sickness.

May Day Parade
May 2, 1948

Yesterday was the big May Day parade, a demonstration of our loyalty and solidarity with the regime. As we were told, we all marched from Teréz korut to Sztalin út, towards Heroes Square. By "all," I mean our class from Ráskai Lea Gimnazium. Apu had to march with the workers of the Forte factory. Panni joined her group of children in the Pioneer Youth Group. We had to wear white blouses and navy skirts, white socks, and red kerchiefs around our necks, the pioneer symbol.

It is really an impressive sight to see the sea of marchers going past the parade stand erected on Heroes Square, with our leaders standing at attention and waving to the loyal citizenry of all ages. President Rákosi was smiling.

The punishment for not attending was a failing grade in social studies at school and a black mark in your father's personnel file, so nobody took that risk.

It is hot, hot, hot. I am very thirsty. Luckily, Nyunyu gave me some lemon drops to put in my pocket in case my mouth got dry.

After we reach the Város liget, my friends Nellie, Zsuzsi, Eva, and I cut out and leave the group. We go to a quiet place across from the zoo and sit and talk. There is a vendor nearby and we buy some lemonade. We congratulate each other for marching so diligently in the parade and following orders, as we should.

We hated our teacher, Zannick Anna, she was so bossy and mean. She had her class list with her, tucked in her shirt, ready to give us a demerit if we did not conform. She is a party informer, and every one tries to avoid her glances. She is dangerous and mean-spirited, and takes actions against all of us on a moment's notice.

Nellie has a new boyfriend. She is really in love and is planning to meet him near the zoo entrance in a little while. Her parents don't know how long the parade will last, so Nellie and her boyfriend are counting on a few private moments together. He has dark hair and is very handsome. He is a senior at the Boys' Academy across the street from our school. They met through the windows. Our classrooms face each other. His name is Feri. They are lovers now.

Must go now! Nyunyu is calling us to supper in the kitchen. The soup smells so delicious.

Living Under Communism

World War II had been terrible for us, but its end, in 1945, introduced another horror. Hungary became part of the Russian-dominated, oppressed Iron Curtain, a satellite of the Soviet Union. This meant that no one could go out or come into Hungary. The borders were guarded by minefields, watchtowers, and soldiers ready to shoot at any moving object. There was no news, no information available from the West. News was only happening in Russia. The world was limited to the Eastern hemisphere. No newspaper, no radio, no communication whatsoever was allowed in Hungary. There was a total oppression of the intellectuals or learned population. Only the children of laborers or peasants were eligible to attend universities or colleges. When you finished high school you were assigned to work on a collective farm somewhere or in a factory production line.

Our vineyards were nationalized, taken over by a government-run farm collective. Stores and banks were nationalized. Private ownership was not permitted. Apartments were appropriated. Families had to move to muddy villages from the city on twenty-four hours' notice. This was called *kilakoltatás*, moving out forcefully.

My father lost his job at the bank because he did not follow the party line. He was assigned an office job at the Forte Factory, a photo supply manufacturer, located about fifty miles north of Budapest. He took a tram there, rain or shine. He was in his late fifties by then. Life was hard and very insecure for us, and the future was dismal.

When my uncle and aunt offered to adopt my sister and me and send us papers to come to the United States, my parents considered accepting their offer. We could not get passports to leave Hungary, so we had to leave illegally, over the minefields with professional smugglers. It was a highly risky and dangerous attempt. The "coyotes," the same type of adventurers who take illegal immigrants across Mexican terrain, knew the layout of the land and had some connection with the border guards to pave our way West.

The story that my parents told the neighbors and police was that they had no knowledge of our whereabouts; I had a boyfriend in the West and it was he who encouraged our leaving Hungary, and it was I who had convinced my thirteen-year-old sister to come along. "Johnny," a boy I had met at a youth rally, was waiting for us somewhere out West. My parents would have been punished otherwise for our illegal border crossing.

After we successfully arrived in Wien (Vienna), my parents felt the weight of loneliness and the breakup of our family, and liquidated their savings to gather the exorbitant sums for the escape, the smugglers' fee. Their story ended in disaster. One of the coyotes got drunk the night before and spilled the beans in a tavern, boasting about their lucrative enterprise. My parents were arrested on exiting the train at the border station of Sopron. My father was beaten on the spot for insubordination. They were taken to the local jail and awaited sentencing for months to come. Their apartment was confiscated and another politically correct family was moved into it right away. They lingered in cold, damp, crowded jails over the winter months. My mother was picked out of the crowd as a cook because she carried her cookbook in her sparse bundle of clothes. She became the prison chef and started dishing out the portions for the hungry prisoners.

Fleeing Across the Border
October 31, 1949

The evening train pulled into the Sopron station. On the platform, waiting and watching the people getting off the second-class compartments, were grey-uniformed, well-armed, steely-eyed border guards. They were looking for anyone carrying heavy luggage or wearing mountain-climbing boots, heavy gear, or raincoats for crossing the fortified Austro-Hungarian border.

"Prepare to show your papers, passports, personal IDs, passes," shouted one guard.

"Border patrol!" shouted the other. "Nobody leaves the station before inspection. Form a single line here!"

My sister and I picked up our bags and put on our raincoats, feeling scared and defenseless. We might have the necessary documents but then how would we find the guides who were to lead us across the minefields? We were pushed and shoved by the restless throng of city people and country folk, all anxious to pass the inspection.

"Why did you travel to Sopron today?" asked the toothless, pockmarked policeman.

"I have to go to the sanatorium for treatment," said my sister, Panni. "I have a heart problem and they will treat me. Here is my doctor's medical statement."

My sister Panni was twelve years old, thin and pale, smaller than most girls her age. I, Ági, was seventeen years old. The guard passed Panni. Now came my turn.

"You, what are you doing here?"

"I am accompanying my sister. Mother had to stay in the city to work."

He checked our documents and let us through. Outside the station we stopped to catch our breaths.

"Whew, that was a close call!" I remember saying.

We looked up to see that the guards who had passed us had arrested two men who did not have the proper documents. The arrested men were handcuffed and marched to a waiting truck. Then we saw a couple, arm in arm, smiling at us. The man tipped his cap politely to attract our attention and then motioned, as if to say, "Follow us. It's OK." We were sure it was Laczi, the guide.

We walked slowly through the town's winding, narrow streets, past small single-family homes. After a while we neared the outskirts, where homes were more neglected and dilapidated. The man pointed to a courtyard and then the couple continued to walk up the street. We looked into the empty enclosure to see a well to the side and a couple of scratching chickens. A woman at a window pulled aside the curtains and then opened the door. We entered a small, darkened room and saw our relatives, Mary and Jenò, sitting in the corner in the shadows.

"Ssh, ssh. Speak in a low voice so that the neighbors won't hear. We have been here two hours already. We are not leaving for the border until midnight. You will need your strength tonight."

We felt good knowing we were not to be alone in our escape. We knew that Mary and Jenò, distant cousins in their thirties, were strong, mature, reliable, and helpful—good company at this difficult time. The hours trickled by slowly. It got darker. We were shown where the outhouse was. We pulled some cheese sandwiches from our handbags, which we ate silently with lukewarm tea. We spoke of our mother, wished she were with us, and fell asleep, a restless sleep with fitful dreams. The cots were narrow and hard. We were tense.

Well into the night the door opened and Laczi, our guide, came in, and whispered, "We are going to start out now. Be sure your shoes are rubber soled so that your footsteps will be quiet."

I quietly switched to my spare shoes. We started out hurriedly, out of the town, into the fields. As we passed the farms, dogs barked angrily. I felt like a fugitive. Panni said she was scared.

"Why do we have to run like this?" she said. "We have not harmed a soul. We have not done anyone wrong. Why do we have to flee like criminals?"

After about an hour's "quick stepping," we came to the border, where searchlights illuminated the terrain.

"You wait in the bushes where it is dark," said Laczi. "I will cut the barbed wire for you to crawl through."

"Good luck," said Jenò, crouching down so as to be close to the ground. We waited. Laczi returned and said, "It's OK now. Come quickly." We followed him to a spot where he held the barbed wire apart so that there was an opening for a small body; a tight squeeze.

"Don't step further. There may be landmines near!" One by one we crawled through the barbed wire fence. I tore my coat out of clumsiness or fear. Soon all five of us were through.

"Don't talk. We are not safe yet," said Laczi in a low voice. "The Hungarians have the right to arrest us within a one-mile radius." Again, we huddled in some dark bushes. Then he said, "The road leads through the woods. Always bear to the right! I will stay with you until we reach the nearest village, Mariahilfe."

We walked and walked. We stumbled on the roots of trees. It was a black, cloudy, moonless night. We walked, we fell, we stumbled some more. The trip through the forest seemed endless. Finally, we asked to rest. Laczi agreed.

"Five minutes only!"

I changed my shoes because my ankles were hurting from the uneven terrain. My sister and I had lemon wedges in our pockets, which quenched our big thirst. Mother had prepared us well for this journey. We kept going. Laczi lent us his arm as he saw exhaustion taking over. It was getting light. The sky was showing us the hope of dawn as we reach the first house in Mariahilfe. We were in Austria, out of the tyranny of Stalin's oppressive regime. The future was ours again.

A Day as a Refugee in Wien, Austria
November 1, 1949

Panni and I had made it through the muddy border, the barking dogs, and the sheer fatigue of walking—walking through the forests with tree roots that we tripped over and soggy leaves that we slipped on. Now we were being delivered to Uncle Alex, our grandfather's old business partner, and his wife, Aunt Trude. They would help us find a place to stay and give us money to live on.

Wien is quiet, few people on the street. It is Sunday, still early. Wien looks a lot like Budapest, only cleaner and brighter. The houses are newly painted and there is no sign of war or bombing anymore. Budapest was so drab, sad, and grey. The houses still showed the remains of bombs and shrapnel craters. But we are free now, out of the Communist noose that choked us. We can speak freely and not worry about spies listening. Wien is occupied by the Allied forces, and we must be very careful not to stray into the Russian zone. The Russians would capture us and deport us back to Hungary.

Our driver stops at an elegant residence, Markt Platz 3/s.

"Das sind sie," he says. "You are here."

How lucky that we speak German fluently. Our parents prepared us for this journey. We get out and ring the bell. After a long wait we gain admittance through the heavy door.

"Este stack," says a young voice. A maid awaits us and motions to us to sit down in the entry hall.

"Die gnadige Frau Kommt schon, bald." "The honored lady will arrive shortly."

We sit and wait. We are tired and scared. Everything is so new to our eyes. We each have only one change of underwear and an extra pair of shoes. We could not carry more over the minefields that separated Hungary from Austria. Our raincoats are torn where we caught them on the barbed wire fence. My sister is thirteen years old and a thin adolescent. I am seventeen, a little chubbier and taller. We look at each other with knowing glances. We have each other and can always count on each other. We are tired and feel unkempt. Aunt Trude arrives in a long blue robe with her entourage of two maids.

"Oh, you are the two girls we heard about. Margaret will serve you breakfast in the parlor and you can wash your hands in the powder room. Uncle Alex is trying to find a room for you where you can stay. There is a small pension nearby. This morning I am very busy. I have to go to my hairdresser. I have a special appointment with her. We are going to the opera tonight. You must excuse me, please."

She leaves in a hurry, picking up the bottom of her long robe as she rushes away. We feel very lonely. We are on our own. Budapest is worlds away and our loving parents a cherished memory. We pick up our bundles and are happy to get breakfast in their elegant dining room.

Babies, Babies, Babies
February 28, 1950

I am at the Kinderhaus at the Rotschild Spital in Wien, Austria. The refugee camp has many babies born to young Holocaust survivors and even to those not so young. It must be Mother Nature's way of replenishing a diminished species to carry on after the horrors of the Holocaust.

I am a nursemaid here, thanks to my friend and protector, Juci Schulz, *Frau* Schulz to the others, who is in charge of the welfare of the arriving Hungarian refugees. The Rotschild Spital is in a now-dilapidated hospital that serves those who have fled illegally with little more than the clothes on their backs. They carried their babies in rucksacks with a change of diapers as they crossed the minefields on the border. Wien is cold and dismal in winter. The Joint Distribution Committee set up this refugee camp under Frau Schulz. We care for the children while their parents await immigration documents.

My charges are little Peter, Moishe, Yingerle, Susanna, and Hildérle. They are each in a crib in one room. When I come in everyone is crying. Whom should I pick up first, to cuddle, feed, or change diapers? Usually I pick up little Peter, Peterke, who pulls my heartstrings.

"Here, here. Don't cry. Tante Ági is here."

He quiets down right away. But the chorus of the others gets louder. The other nursemaid, Tante Trude, picks up her favorite, Hildérle. Peterke has a runny nose and dirty diapers. The babies are six to eight months old, too young to be away from their parents but safer here, where it is clean and well maintained, rather than in the *lager,* a camp for refugees, where infections and active tuberculosis are rampant, sanitation is poor, toilets are shared, and there are head lice and other pests. Parents come in often to hold their babies for a while. When they see their baby's nursemaid, they ask for details, how their youngster is doing.

At the central kitchen we pick up cooked oatmeal and sterilized bottles for the babies. We have a toddler program too, where the children sit at low tables and color and draw. A teacher comes in to sing with them. Some are just learning to speak, and German is not their mother tongue. I speak Hungarian to Peterke, whose parents are from Budapest. Tante Trude speaks in German to Hildérle, who comes from a border city on the Austrian border. It is quite international here. Moishe comes from Yiddish-speaking parents who fled from Poland. Another staff member is Czech. But all of the staff speak enough German to get along perfectly well and do our jobs. I love these children and am protective of them. This is my first job. I have been away from home for only three months. Working here makes me feel important, as someone who makes a difference in these lives. I hold them and they nurture me.

Being a refugee in a strange country is lonely. My sister, Panni, and I live in the apartment of an old lady. The place is so cold that the old lady stays in bed to keep warm. Luckily she has a gentleman friend who helps her keep warm. We don't have much money so we cannot change our living situation. I earn only a small amount of money. Our Uncle Andy sends funds sporadically. Meanwhile, Panni spends her days in a school where they keep the students until late afternoon. It is in Hitzing, a suburb of Wien. She has to take a train but she gets good dinners there.

We walk on the boulevards in the early evening to get acquainted with our new city and to visit other refugees whom we know from home. Panni is very close to our distant cousins, the Hébers—Józsi and Julcsi—and their two-year-old girl Katyi. I am happiest when we get an invitation from Juci Schulz. She is my role model because she is realistic about the welfare of others and tries to improve their lives.

Soon we will go to a convent in Paris where we will await our entrance visas to the United States. Life is full of adventure and we are ready for the unexpected.

Paris
April 9, 1950

This is the first time that my sister, Panni, and I have flown on an airplane. We are flying from Wien, Austria, to Paris, France.

We had crossed the border between Hungary and Austria just six months before. In Wien we established our stateless status and were helped by international organizations to get clothing and food. Our uncle in America has been pulling strings to get us admitted into the United States as non-quota immigrants by legally adopting us. In the meantime, he feels we will be safer while we wait in a Catholic convent, a school for girls, in Paris, rather than on our own. At that time Wien was occupied by the Allied forces, including the Russians, and one could easily walk into danger if one got lost on the winding streets of the old city.

So here we are, two wide-eyed girls in our only nice outfits, which we have been wearing since leaving our family home in Budapest: grey wool suits with white blouses, brown shoes, white socks, gloves, and nicely tailored brown purses. Ages seventeen and thirteen, we wonder what Paris will have in store for us.

At the airport gate two people are awaiting us: our parents' friend, Aunt Lili, who had also migrated recently to France, and an elderly nun, Sister Joseph, from the convent where we are to reside and study French.

Sister Joseph is very thin and frail. We notice her skinny arm, exposed when she lifts her black habit. Aunt Lili, by contrast, is wearing several gold bracelets and necklaces, and her hair is styled in what we guess to be the latest Parisian fashion. A taxi waits for us, and shortly we are on our way to Boulogne-sur-Seine, outside of Paris near the Bois de Boulogne, where the sister's convent is located.

It is night by then and my sister and I are enraptured by the dazzling bright electric lights of Paris. We drive along the river Seine, where we see vendors' stalls and the Eiffel tower, and in the distance the bridges float by like lovely necklaces.

Such beauty. Such splendor. We are so excited to be here. We are seeing the big world that we had previously seen only in picture books.

Then the lights fade and we drive on dark country roads to arrive at a formidable brick structure, the convent and church of the Sisters of St. Joseph. Our German-speaking nun rings an old fashioned bell and a young, small sister opens the door.

"Mother Superior is awaiting you," she says.

We are led into a sparsely furnished office containing a desk, large chairs, and a lamp. Mother Superior enters. She is tall with a humorless, stoic expression on her face.

"You must be the refugee girls Father Dominic, from our church in Illinois, wrote us about. We will accept you here as our students and Sister Joseph will give you daily French instruction. You will sleep in the dormitories with the other girls, share their washroom, and keep your trunks near your beds. We all dine in the common dining hall. Dismissed for now!"

Sister Joseph takes us with a flashlight to a large dormitory, where twenty or so girls are snoring. We say goodbye to Aunt Lili and to our freedom, able no more to act on our own, without rules and regulations.

Panni weeps all night. I fall asleep from sheer exhaustion. The bright lights of Paris are no longer shining for us.

Three Months Later

Panni and I followed the rules that Mother Superior imposed on us.

We got used to rising early, going to the big washroom with rows of sinks that provided cold water splashes on our sleepy faces, and the weekly hot showers taken communally on Saturday. We filed in two neat rows to the dining hall, sat at long rectory-style tables, and ate our oatmeal mush and drank lukewarm sweet tea for breakfast.

We went for walks with the other girls to the Bois de Boulogne. We skipped rope, played hopscotch, and tried to communicate with the others in simple words. We had our daily French lessons and later giggled with each other at all the oddities we observed. The girls wore such loose pajamas in bed and wore white knee-stockings under their pleated skirts that got grey after a week's use.

The convent was cold and damp, though the air outside turned from spring to summer. We could go out only when Aunt Lili picked us up, and it was not often. The convent was out of town and taxis were expensive. But on those rare occasions we were in constant amazement at how beautiful Paris looked. We saw the Arc de Triomphe, the Victory arch from which all the boulevards fanned out like a star. We saw the Musée Louvre and walked in the gardens nearby. We promenaded on the wide boulevard, the Champs-Élysées, and looked into the shop windows. The styles of clothing dazzled our eyes. Women looked chic and elegant in their high heels and short skirts. We wished we could dress like them.

But soon it was time to get back to the convent for supper.

We filed in with the other girls for the dinner bell. This evening the meal consisted of one large artichoke.

"We have never seen such a plant before. How do you eat it?" we asked.

They showed us.

"Put your knife across the plate. Tip the artichoke and balance it on it. Put some oil and vinegar on the edge of your plate. Pull off the leaves one by one. Dip a leaf into the oil and voilà, a delicious bite is yours. Keep on going till you reach the choke. Remove the fuzzy part and the rest is all edible."

Alas. We still had hunger pangs when we were all done. Luckily there were seconds on bread.

When we went up to our dorm room, we saw that our trunks were open and our clothes were thrown about. On closer inspection we noticed that our mother's gold necklace, rings, and bracelets, some of the precious family heirlooms that we had carried with us for safekeeping from Wien, wrapped in a scarf and hidden in a purse under our linens, were gone. We were shocked and upset. We had been burglarized and vandalized. We ran to Mother Superior and asked her to call the police.

"A crime has been committed. We can never replace these precious items."

She listened, then said sternly, "Of course we will look into this matter but we don't ever involve the police. Whatever goes on in this convent is in our jurisdiction. Calling the police would create adverse publicity for our school."

The next day Mother Superior asked us to prepare our trunks. We were moved to another facility for homeless young girls. Our presence at this convent caused "too much conflict," she said.

The jewels were never returned. It was a loss and a disappointment we carried with us through the decades. We still wonder who could have taken them. After all, this was supposed to be such a safe place.

My Birthday in Paris
July 7, 1950

Yesterday was my eighteenth birthday. I feel so grown up. Andy Slovak sent a friend to visit us. His name is Franz Petritz. He is a friend of the Slovaks. He lives in Rockford and he is in Paris on a tour. So he came on my birthday and brought us gifts from Andy and Sylvia. We got a box of chocolates. They were so delicious. And I got a camera, my very own camera, with five rolls of film. Now I can take pictures of all the fabulous sights in Paris. I am practicing at first and taking artistic shots of Panni in the convent garden. She looks so pretty as the sun illuminates her profile. Panni is fourteen years old now and is developing into a beautiful young lady. We do fight a lot still, mostly about possessions and money. We have so little money and very few cosmetic items. She takes better care of soap and toothpaste than I do, also of hairpins and curlers, and she won't lend any to me when I am in need. We always make up soon after our verbal battles.

We miss our family terribly—Nyunyu, Apu, and Grandfather. They are still behind the Iron Curtain, and letters don't arrive because the censors are brutal and strict: neither news nor complaints can come out to the West from the Iron Curtain. Nevertheless, we learned that Nyunyu and Apu, who had been caught while trying to escape after our own escape, had gotten out of jail and were living in a rented room on the Liszt Ferency ter. Apu will soon have a prostate operation. They survived the awful conditions in prison even though Apu is unwell and needs medical treatment. That was the reason their sentence was reduced. The Communists were afraid that Apu might die in jail, so the judge chose to be merciful. We can just hope and pray that they will both get back on their feet.

Arrival in the U.S.
October 14, 1950

"Fasten your seat belts," announced the smiling, blonde stewardess on the TWA flight from Paris to Chicago. "We are landing at the Chicago O'Hare Airport."

Ann (Panni) was thirteen years old and Agnes (Ági) had just turned eighteen. (They had decided to use the American versions of their names.) Their maternal uncle Andy and his wife, Sylvia, had adopted them. Sylvia was Danish by ancestry and her mother, Sofia, lived with them in Rockford, Illinois.

Andy Slovak had been born and raised in Budapest and had left Hungary during his college years, in 1918, because of an anti-Semitic attack that he had endured at the university. A group of nationalistic hoodlums had come into his class and asked, "Who is a Jew here?" He stood, and they beat him up. Blood flowed. He never returned to the university after that. His mother got his credentials and papers. Andy left to study abroad and got his diploma at the Charlottenburg University, in Berlin. Later, in 1924, he sailed to New York and joined the family of his Uncle Elmer. He tried to erase his Hungarian background and his Jewish identity. He became a patriotic American and a hard-working engineer. Years later he married his boss's daughter, Sylvia, and they settled in Rockford after he had taken a job there with Ingersoll Machinery. By 1950 Andy owned and operated a screw-machine company, Unit Machinery. He and his wife were prosperous citizens of the town, members of the country club, the Rotary club, and the First Methodist Church.

Agnes and Ann had survived the Holocaust, the siege of Budapest, liberation by the Russian troops, the slow recovery period after the city emerged from the ruins, and later, the takeover by the Communist regime. Rákosi had become the prime minister, the handpicked hatchet man of Stalin. It was because of this dictatorial, terrorist regime that the two sisters fled over the minefields, crossing the Austro-Hungarian border on foot at night. Their parents, Nyunyu and Apu, had hired two reliable border-crossing smugglers to take the sisters to the safety of Wien, which was under Allied control at the time, and from there they would go to Paris, where they would await their journey to America.

And now they were on their way. The two young girls fastened their seatbelts and whispered a short prayer, "Dear God, help us at this new phase of our lives. May we understand what they are telling us, and may we accept what is expected of us in this new, strange place called America."

As they got to the gate, two smiling people waited for them and greeted them, waving heartily.

"Hi! You must be Agnes, and you, young lady, must be Ann. Welcome to America. I am Andy Daddy," said the tall, heavy-set man.

"And I am your Sylvia Mommy," said the blonde, excited woman.

"Sylvia Mommy" had been the youngest child and only daughter of a Danish emigrant family. Her parents, Sofia and Soren, came from Randers, Denmark, in the early twentieth century. Soren was a machine-tool maker and owned his own tool-making factory in Cincinnati, Ohio. The Cincinnati Gear Company had prospered and was still in business, one hundred years later. Sylvia had studied to be a teacher. She was a very conscientious kindergarten teacher when she met Andy and they married. She was blonde, winsome, and plump, very much in love with the red-haired, volatile-tempered immigrant boy from Hungary. Sylvia and Andy had two babies who died after birth because of the Rh factor—their blood types were incompatible and could not be treated in the 1930s. Sylvia was hoping to become a mother by adopting Agnes and Ann, their nieces. She was not a demonstrative, outgoing person, but reserved and preachy, or schoolmarmish, in her approach with the girls. Her guideline was to provide a good educational climate for them with a Protestant work ethic and all-American values. She often said, "If you work hard and play hard, you will get ahead." Sylvia herself was the vice president and comptroller of Andy's tool and screw manufacturing plant. She controlled the purse strings. Andy tended to be more impulsive.

"First we'll go through customs when your suitcases arrive, and then we'll take you to our car."

The customs officers showed great curiosity in the gold jewelry that they carried in a pouch with them. The few pieces of jewelry they had left were now in their purses as keepsakes—necklaces, rings, and bracelets that had belonged to their mother and were to be used as emergency resale property. They had gone through many episodes where cash had to be generated for unforeseen reasons. At this very moment their parents were in prison somewhere in Hungary for their unsuccessful attempt to cross the same border that the two girls had crossed. The parents had once thought the sale of the jewelry might hasten their release from prison.

Soon their small, weather-beaten bags arrived. They were packed into the trunk of the car and off they went, Andy Daddy at the helm of his new, spacious Cadillac sedan. Agnes and Ann had never seen such a comfortable car before and had never ridden in such luxury.

Instead of going straight home, to Rockford, about eighty miles from the Chicago airport, Sylvia Mommy informed them that first they would stop at a mushroom farm, because "that would be an educational experience for the girls." Well, they were tired and felt dirty after the twenty-hour flight, but smilingly they marched along the rows of cultivated mushrooms in various stages of development, then back into the car.

Andy then announced, "We need to eat lunch, since we are still a long way from home." So they stopped at a diner, another new, all-American experience for the girls. They sat on stools reading an incomprehensible menu. They were not familiar with hamburgers or cheeseburgers. Even Coca-Cola was something exotic and unfamiliar to them. They ate fruit salad with cottage cheese. It tasted sweet and felt cooling and comforting. It was here that they heard Andy Daddy first speak Hungarian: *"Ez túró."* "This is cottage cheese." They dozed off soon in the car after lunch.

When they reached Rockford, Andy Daddy pulled the car into the driveway of a palatial home, a mansion in their eyes, on the corner of Harlem Boulevard. At the door they were embraced by Sylvia's eighty-six-year-old mother, Grandmother Sofia. Sofia Sorensen was a neatly coiffed, wrinkled, smiling, kind old woman. She had lived with Andy and Sylvia since the death of her husband Soren Sorensen. She had a private bedroom and bathroom off the kitchen. She was very proud of the fact that she was the family's cook and had a meal ready every night in spite of her eighty-six years.

"You must be so tired. Come in and freshen up. I have been waiting for you for hours."

They were shown their bedroom and their own private bathroom upstairs. They were overwhelmed by the spaciousness and comforts offered to them but they were also tired, exhausted, and in need of some rest and time to sort out their newfound family and the expectations awaiting them in Rockford, Illinois, in the middle of the United States, where nobody spoke their mother tongue. It was all so strange and new. They were captives in a gilded cage, and they tried to sing a happy song.

My First Job in the New World
January 3, 1951

The snow was piled in six-foot-high banks on the two sides of State Street as Mrs. Garthe gingerly drove her white Oldsmobile and pulled into the doctors' parking lot at St. Anthony's Hospital. I sat in the passenger seat and remained silent through the short trip.

I was worried about what I would find at my new job. I was going to be a nurse's aide in the newborn nursery unit, right next to the busy delivery room. Our family friend, Mrs. Garthe, whose husband was one of the staff doctors, got me the original job interview with Miss Kegel, the head nurse. She asked about my experience, which I told her was in a refugee camp in Vienna. The children we cared for needed mothering, cuddling, and some nourishing meals. They were separated from their parents and were cold, lonely, and forlorn. I had wondered to myself: how was I to translate those intuitive job skills, learned in a makeshift, old-fashioned set up, and manage a new job in a modern American hospital? Before I could find an answer I was directed to a staff locker room where I exchanged my street clothes for a white uniform, a cap, and protective shoe covers. I had to scrub my hands and report to the floor supervisor. Miss Matthews told me my job was to bathe the newborn infants, powder their bottoms, gently brush their hair, and record the contents of their diapers, urine or stool, and its color.

I saw the nursery finally. The babies were placed in rows of sparkling chrome bassinets, with fragrant, newly washed linens still warm from the sterilizing effects of the autoclave.

From there they were taken to the rows of changing tables. The supplies were within easy reach—cotton swabs, baby oil, dusting powder, washcloths, and soft towels.

I was not sure how to pick up those tiny babies with their flopping heads. I was shown how to support their necks and hold the backs of their heads in my left palm while I washed them with my right hand. After handling three newborns the job started to feel easier. The babies didn't break so easily. I found that they were individuals and they each responded in their own way to my gentle efforts. Some cried as if I were skinning them alive. I tried to talk to them, to reassure them that it was all right and soon they would be back in their cribs safely; I shushed the little darlings. Others wiggled and tried to get out of my hands. These I held more firmly and my voice was a little more commanding, telling them to hold on for a while. The time went by so fast I was amazed when shortly I was told to go on a break.

The next day I was allowed to feed the preemies. Some babies, born prematurely, were kept in incubators, and little three-ounce feeding bottles were heated up for them. These babies were already five or six pounds and could be lifted up without any oxygen tubes attached. There was a rocking chair that we were told to sit in, and the babies could be cuddled and rocked while feeding. This was a job for me. I loved holding those fragile little ones.

One day a baby was born with a birth defect. The skull bone did not close properly and the skin did not cover the opening. I only peeked from the corner of my eye at this dear little creature, struggling to survive. I was not permitted to touch this infant. Miss Kegel took complete charge of it. This baby lived for only three days, and when it died I was told to deliver it to the morgue wrapped in a blanket. On that day I hated my new job.

Then another dramatic event shook us up. One of the mothers had a brain embolism a few hours after delivering a healthy baby girl. When I took the baby to her room so she could look at it and hold it after the baby's initial bath, she told me that she felt dizzy and the room was going round. Luckily I reported this to Miss Kegel, who called a doctor to look in on her. Soon the crash cart was rushed to her room. We had an orphaned baby girl in the nursery that day. It broke my heart to look at her.

Later on I was shown how to prepare a baby for circumcision. There was a board that the baby boys were strapped onto with their genitals exposed for the quick procedure. The only anesthesia was a cube of sugar wrapped in a square of gauze, dipped into sterile water. With all the compassion I could muster, I tried to hold them straight and pray the doctor would be quick in attaching a clamp and snipping off the foreskin. Those babies deserved extra soothing lullabies afterwards. They all recovered from their surgery. I soon realized that some doctors have magic hands and others are bumbling incompetents. I also learned that the nursing profession is to be admired because they are the healers of the sick and the providers of the medical care that doctors too routinely and often carelessly prescribe. Nurses question the dosage of pills when needed and often prevent catastrophes.

The sight of blood, deformity, and death ultimately deterred me from becoming a nurse, but the year I spent in the nursery certainly prepared me for the challenge of motherhood. I bathed my three baby sons with expert hands. And I was never ashamed to take time to cuddle them afterwards. Some lessons are not to be forgotten.

Sudden Impact
Rockford, 1951

She did not like it when I borrowed her personal things. She always kept her drawers neat and her cosmetics wrapped in tissue paper. Her earrings were in neat boxes, and her necklaces were lined up in the bottom of her velvet-lined jewelry case. Combs, brushes, and hairspray were lined up on the bathroom shelves like soldiers, with makeup, lipstick, and eye shadow right below. My sister was fourteen years old. She was neat, tidy, and adamant about her privacy and self-sufficiency. After all, she bought all this adult paraphernalia with her allowance. My sister got fifty cents a week and I, four years older, got a whopping quarter more. We spent money differently. I preferred to buy books and writing paper.

Everything was new and different here. The life that American teenagers lived was mysterious to us both. Girls here used makeup at fourteen: rouge, lipstick, and eye shadow. Back where we came from, this was not customary. The fresh-scrubbed look was admired there, and the use of cosmetics was delegated to the more mature, more seductive, and less pristine types of girls than we were.

One day a boy asked me to go to the movies. He was a freshman at the college I attended. Richard Brown was my first date in the new country. I was excited and quite nervous about going out with him. Richard had curly brown hair and soft brown eyes. What should I wear? How should I look? I wanted to look grown up. I had no tools to make myself look good. I decided to borrow my sister's eyebrow pencil, cheek blush, and lip-gloss. I snuck them out of her cosmetic line up when she was not in the room. I worked quickly and was amazed at the results. These things actually worked! My eyes looked prettier and my cheeks were blushed. I was all set to go downstairs to meet Richard.

Just then my sister came up to the room. Seeing me all made up she screamed, "You took my stuff! How dare you use my things!" She snatched her makeup out of my hand. She wiped the lipstick off my amazed lips, erasing my smile from my face. She slapped my right cheek. She slapped my left. I was really red now. The imprint of her fingers left marks on my rouged cheeks.

Our Wedding Day (September 19, 1954) and Young Married Years

"Wedding bells are ringing for Agnes Kathelin Biró and Isaiah L. Rothblatt on September 19, 1954. Agnes has just graduated from the University of Wisconsin (Madison) with a B.A. degree in social work. Agnes is the daughter of Mr. and Mrs. Andrew Slovak, Rockford, Illinois. She is a member of the Gamma Phi Beta sorority. Isaiah received his M.S. (social work) degree in June from the University of Wisconsin (Madison). He is the son of Benjamin and Clara Rothblatt, of Madison, Wisconsin. He is a veteran of World War II and a captain in the U.S. Army Reserves. He will be assuming a social work position at Southern Colony Hospital in Union Grove, Wisconsin, this September. The young couple plan to live in Racine, Wisconsin, after returning from a honeymoon in New Orleans, Louisiana. Bridesmaids will be the bride's sister, Ann Marie Biró, and the groom's sister, Anita Rothblatt. The wedding dinner will be held at the Edgewater Hotel in Madison, Wisconsin."

This was the announcement that appeared in the *Wisconsin State Journal*. With this matter-of-fact report, most people did not suspect the details that were left out. The wedding ceremony was held at the home of the university Hillel Foundation rabbi and his wife, Max and Esther Ticktin. It was a lovely, simple Jewish ceremony with Rabbi Ticktin giving a soulful and heartfelt blessing to his friends, the bride, and groom.

The bride had survived the Holocaust in Hungary and was able to come to America when she was adopted by her maternal uncle and aunt in Rockford, Illinois. But their orientation and

70

social status made it awkward for them to host a Jewish wedding in Rockford, thus the present arrangement. The groom, known as Shike, had been in combat not only in Europe, at the Battle of the Bulge, but also with the Israeli Army during their War of Independence, in 1948 and 1949. After the State of Israel was established on May 15, 1948, Shike had volunteered to join the effort. He stayed on for a while after the fighting to become better acquainted with relatives who had migrated to Israel from Russia and Poland after the end of World War II.

At their wedding, in Madison, they stood under a makeshift *chuppah* with a few carefully chosen posies. The bride wore a light blue taffeta dress. The bridesmaids accompanied her, one wearing jade green, the other deep raspberry matching gowns. They looked young, fresh, and beautiful. The traditional glass was broken, champagne cork popped, and the celebration was on its way. Dinner at the Edgewater Hotel was elegant and dignified, with a shocking moment when the bride and her sister ate the trout entrée completely, fish eyes and all, an old Hungarian custom. The assistant bartender was the groom's thirteen-year-old brother, Andy, already multi-talented, and when the occasion called for it, a comedian as well as a bartender. The guests were just close family: Shike's parents; brothers, David and Andy; sister, Anita; and cousins from Cleveland, Sonia and Sam Tepper, along with their three daughters, Eileen, Edie, and Cindy. Agnes's roommate, Eileen, was also there. The best man, Raffie (Raul) Stern, and his wife, Ruth (Danie, for her homeland, Denmark), graced the wedding table.

After the wedding dinner, the newlyweds drove off on a stormy night in their 1950 Ford, trailing old shoes and cans behind, to their new apartment in Racine.

Ági and Shike had met at the university hospital where they both worked weekends as attendants. The university hired students to supplement their staff. Ági worked as a floater, where the staff needed supplementation, often at the orthopedic ward, where recovering polio patients were convalescing. The polio vaccine was a new discovery but the ravages of the disease were still present. Ági formed warm relationships and meaningful contacts with these young people who were trying to get back on their feet and were getting physiotherapy there. Shike worked in the psych ward with patients who needed personal care and also were in need of socializing. He played cards with them, lucky guy. Good job for a social worker.

Ági and Shike dated for close to two years in Madison, while Ági lived in the dorms and the sorority house under strict curfew. Shike lived with his parents and siblings. David worked at Gisholt, then a factory, and drove nice cars. He was generous to let his brother Shike borrow these on special dates with Ági.

Ági was active in the campus International Club, where members took turns cooking ethnic meals for the group. Ági volunteered to give a goulash party and Shike helped her with the posters, the shopping, even entertaining the guests while the big pot of goulash slowly bubbled to perfection. Ági had never cooked for such a large crowd before.

Shike's family welcomed Ági to their family events—*Shabbat* dinners, Passover celebrations—and made her feel part of their circle. Ági in turn helped to paint the inside of their house, along with the Rothblatt sons—up and down the ladders and sometimes paint all over. A marriage made not only in heaven but down to earth. A good start for the decades to come!

Life as a Newlywed
October 19, 1954

We settled into the first home of our month-old marriage at 800 S. Main Street in Racine, Wisconsin, a city of about 80,000 inhabitants, on Lake Michigan. Our apartment was on the second floor of a chopped-up Victorian, a high-ceilinged studio with a large main room and a walk-through closet leading to the kitchen. We painted the kitchen glossy sunflower, which looked beautiful as a sample but was overwhelming in the large, sunlit kitchen. The bay windows of the main room faced east, across a busy tree-lined boulevard, toward a white funeral parlor with a large parking lot. Just beyond was the lake. We lived in a great neighborhood. The mansion-sized homes along our boulevard (really a main street) had deep lawns, and we were but a few blocks from the city center.

We parked our recently purchased 1950 Ford in front of the house. It served us well on our honeymoon to New Orleans, four days' driving each way. We had already driven it a lot. For our wedding night, we drove from Madison to Racine, pulling a trailer with our few belongings. It was an adventure in itself. We had since visited Uncle Andy and Aunt Sylvia in Rockford, Illinois. We had driven to our sister city, Kenosha, eight miles away and also visited nearby Milwaukee. That city had become our most frequent destination because of its cultural activities, family relations, and variety of shopping possibilities. New Orleans was my first long car trip. I had been apprehensive about traveling to the South because of its troubling legends of racism.

The honeymoon trip to New Orleans was indeed memorable. The car performed well but our time on the road was bewildering with its distances, varied terrain, contrasting towns, evident poverty, and my apprehensions. My fears faded as we encountered unwavering friendliness, characterized by waitresses greeting us with "honey" and charm.

We found a nice motel there. Shike's relatives, Rose and Morrie Sweig, made us feel welcome. They lived on Robert E. Lee Boulevard. He operated a furniture store and they had a pretty five-year-old, Rachael, with long, blonde curly hair. We had a plentiful *Shabbat* dinner at their old-fashioned home. We visited famous restaurants in the French quarter, and I ate shellfish and crab for the first time.

Unfortunately, I came down with a skin rash when we entered New Orleans, very itchy and red, all over my body. Was I allergic to my husband? Shike took me to a doctor, who diagnosed an allergy to some local plant. I suspected the touching and smelling of oleanders in the motel parking lot and, indeed, the prescribed cream seemed to improve my condition.

Back at Main Street, all was new. It felt like the foundation of an exciting and long life, as it has turned out to be. I remember our first shopping trip on Sixth Street. Shike helped carry bags. As I planned to cook more, we got all the essential staples, such as flour, eggs, milk, jam, oil, cold cuts, a cut-up chicken, and onions. We spent seven dollars. Rent was $80, which we paid to Mr. Christianson, the caretaker of the house, which was owned by a doctor.

Shike drove daily to Southern Colony, a state institution for the developmentally disabled in Union City, thirty miles away. I was looking for work. I had an interview for a part-time sales job at Lads and Lassies, a children's clothing store, further down on Main Street, about eight blocks from our apartment. I had not done sales before, but I had been a waitress and I like to work with people and really like working with children.

Our college friend Phyllis Finkel lived in Kenosha, eight miles from Racine and similar in size. We planned to see her that weekend. Phyllis was a social worker at the welfare department. She had been a teaching assistant in an anthropology course I took the previous summer in Madison. Our other college friend, Vern Haubrich, was then working at American Motors in Kenosha.

We watched our budget, having exhausted our savings in setting up house and taking the big trip. Shike's income covered basic expenses and left a bit for savings and some luxuries like clothes and eating out, but we had to be careful in our expenditures.

It was really fine to be independent and starting a new life. I was a happy new bride and hoped the honeymoon would continue for a long time.

I missed my sister, Panni, being far from her now, and I especially worried about my parents, still imprisoned by the Communists in Budapest. Panni had started college at the University of Wisconsin, in Madison, and liked it. We telephoned and wrote each other frequently. America is such a big place, with its people scattered, not like back in Budapest, where we could walk to each other's homes.

Nyunyu Arrives
October 14, 1957

When I answered the telephone one day in October 1957, the friendly voice of cousin Leni's husband, Walter Morris, announced, "Somebody here would like to talk to you!" It was my dear mother, our Nyunyuka, who had just arrived in New York after eight years of separation from me.

In October 1949, after my sister, Panni, and I took the train to the border of Hungary to flee the country, we were followed a few weeks later by our parents, except they were arrested and imprisoned for the crime of trying to leave the country without any documents, after the smugglers spilled the facts to the secret police. After many months in brutal prisons, they returned to Budapest, only to lose their home and be forced to live with strangers in crowded quarters; they suffered the privations and repressions of the Stalinist regime for years. In 1956 the failed Hungarian revolution brought about some easing of government controls. When it was announced that the older adults would be given passports to leave the country, our mother, Nyunyu, was the first in line to apply. Our father, Apu, age sixty-six, felt too old and sick to start a new life across the ocean and chose to stay in his well-known surroundings in Budapest, alone.

Nyunyu spent a year in Wien as a refugee, awaiting her American visa, which finally was issued. She embarked on a refugee transport ship, the *Vulcania*, to come to the New World. Her two cousins, Leni and Lotte, waited for her at the New York pier and they instantly recognized each other. Leni's car was waiting, the suitcases were packed into the trunk, and off they went to Englewood, New Jersey, to the Fenyvesy Morris residence. Aunt Lisbeth, the *mater familias*, greeted them and prepared a delicious welcome meal. The "girls" talked until 3 a.m. catching up on all the family news.

When we finally spoke on the phone a few hours later, Nyunyu was still very excited but a little calmer about her arrival to the United States.

"Ágikam, can it be true that we are talking to each other after all these years? And that we will soon see each other! You are a married woman now, with a nice husband, and you live in your own home, which I will see when I come to stay with you. I am so excited I can hardly wait."

Two days later, on a stormy, wintry November evening, Nyunyu landed at the Milwaukee airport in her elegant raincoat and matching hat and was embraced not only by Shike and me, but also by my sister, Panni, and her fiancé, Roger, as well as by her brother, Andy Slovak, and his wife, Sylvia. It was a very happy and emotional reunion.

Dinner was ready when they arrived at Ági and Shike's home—baked ham, mashed potatoes, green beans, and a chocolate torte, Sacher style. The past had to be remembered and preserved. At least gastronomically, Nyunyu was home again.

The Reunion

Ann was thirteen when she came to live with her new parents in Illinois, and she adapted fully. She learned English and she became the daughter her new parents had hoped for. She was popular at school, had new friends, and got good grades.

Agnes was a bit more resistant to the new life. She preferred to speak her native language, especially to her sister. She looked for Hungarian friends and she resented her adoptive parents' advice that she attend Methodist Sunday services with them. She found it difficult to let go of her old ways. At college she sought the company of other foreign students who faced the issues of newcomers in the United States.

After school, Ann married a golf pro, who was also a Top Ten collegiate athlete, and who grew up in a country club and showed great promise for a successful career.

Agnes chose a social worker, who found a job in an institution for the retarded in rural Wisconsin.

As the car rolled on and passed landmarks near the airport, Ann said, "I can't believe it, that we will finally be reunited with our dear mother. She has been through so much in these intervening years. She was arrested as she first crossed the border. She spent years in jail, where she ended up as the jail's cook. She got a job as a seamstress in a sweatshop, followed by illness and hospitalization, and finally escape from the oppressive socialist government. These years must have left terrible marks on her body and soul. She must have suffered and she must have aged and been crushed by all the hardships. We have not had a letter from her for years, until the phone call came from the Joint Refugee organization, saying that she had arrived safely in Wien, Austria, after a successful escape over the Hungarian border. I, too, wonder what she looks like now. I remember her as a beautiful, well-groomed, and elegantly dressed young woman, whose eyes sparkled as she spoke. Her bracelets jangled as she walked, she never stood still, always did something, noticed everything, and she was there to take care of every detail in the house or in our nursery."

"I didn't think that we would ever see her again," said Agnes. "I have wept bitter tears many a night with the fear of losing her behind the Iron Curtain. I am so nervous I almost cannot wait. I am also thinking of our dinner cooking back at the house and hope it will still be edible when we get home."

Their car pulled into the parking lot of the airport. They arrived at the gate. The plane was on time in spite of the bad weather. The passengers deplaned slowly. At the very end of the procession was their mother, head held high, smiling, nicely outfitted in a plaid raincoat with matching hat, walking erect, even proudly, as she warmly embraced her two grown-up daughters.

"Isten hozott," said Agnes. "God brought you safely, *szervusztok. Gyerekek.*"

"Hello, my children."

Their life together was starting anew. The last eight years disappeared in this instant of mutual embrace.

A Move
June 15, 1959

I was soaking in the bathtub. The temperature in Racine was 95 degrees. I felt relaxed and comfortable at last. We had finally fixed our home the way we liked it: painted the walls beige and the ceiling sky blue; covered the old couch with rosy chintz; put the family pictures on the wall.

I relished the aroma of the chestnut bath gel as I turned on the hot water tap to fill the tub to the rim. Ah, life can be beautiful.

A knock on the door.

"Are you in there, Ági?" my husband asked. "I have great news for you. I've just opened the mail and I was hired for the children's home job in San Francisco. We are moving to California! We will be living on the grounds of Homewood Terrace and I'll be the residential director."

I was shocked at first. Why now, when we had finally gotten settled in Racine? Leave our cozy home for some strange institution? Go to a city that we barely know, somewhere on the West Coast, practically at the end of the world?

But my realistic mind got the better of me. I got my large bath towel, dried myself, and gave my husband a hug.

Our Baby Turns One
December 31, 1959

Today is our Danny's first birthday. He was born in snowy, stormy Racine, Wisconsin. We carried him home wrapped in warm, snuggly blankets, amidst high mountains of snow on the road. Now we are in rainy but temperate California.

What big changes in our lives! We live in a children's home, Homewood Terrace, in San Francisco, California. Shike is the assistant director here, on call many a night, to take care of unruly, runaway children. He has to bring them back, or if they were involved in mischief, he has to follow them to "Juvie"— Juvenile Hall—where they will spend their punishment under lock and key. We live in a spacious house on the grounds of the children's home. There is a private bedroom and bath for Nyunyu, who moved to California with us. We have another bedroom and bath at the other wing of this lovely house and there is a smaller room for our baby, Dan. In the middle of the house is the entryway, the dining room, and a living room with a big fireplace. The kitchen and pantry are in back. How lucky can we be? Food is ordered weekly, just by writing the shopping list and calling it in to Art Weil, the maintenance supervisor.

Nyunyu bakes us wonderful cookies and made a delicious sponge cake filled with strawberry jam for our baby's first birthday. She has decorated it with whipping cream.

Danny is a big boy for his age, strong and agile. He is curious about the world around him. He can talk now. I take him to the lawn behind our house and he takes big steps as he picks the flowers. He has beautiful, curly brown hair. Soon he will need his first haircut. He expresses himself so well. He can say, "Mama," "Dada," "no," "more," and he nods his head if he wants something. He is such a smart boy. We are so proud of him.

We are going to have a small birthday party for him. Our friends Helen and Dan Rosenblat are coming. Howard and Paula Margolis promised to make it from Berkeley. Cousin Cookie Roitblat is bringing a "big toy" for Danny and asked us to pick her up at the streetcar stop. She is our only local relative, a schoolteacher in Oakland. She moved here after she finished college in Madison, Wisconsin.

The Rosenblats are new friends for me. Dan and Shike were in the U.S. Army together, and they had stayed in touch all these years. Dan is a specialist in the stock market. Helen is his tall, attractive wife. They are so sophisticated and elegant. Howard Margolis was Shike's social work school buddy. They had the same field-work placement in Janesville, Wisconsin, and shared a ride to and from Madison. He is an eccentric guy. He likes to play silly jokes on people. Paula is his lovely, German-born wife. She takes care of babies in her own nursery in their home. They have a son, Paulie, who is two years old. Paula gives us his outgrown baby clothes. Danny is wearing the short blue pants that they gave us recently. He looks so cute in them! I consider Howie and Paula to be bohemians, nonconformists. Howard works as a social worker now in a rehab center. Cookie went to school with me. We were in the same psychology class. Professor Thurlow was our teacher. Cookie is smart but she is a high-strung, nervous person.

Shike is not on duty today, which is wonderful because it is New Year's Eve and the Homewood kids will be highly charged and ready to act up. I plan to open a bottle of champagne when our guests arrive. We have reason to celebrate. Our lives are on a good track and we are happy.

Homewood Terrace, 1960

Homewood Terrace is a world of its own. Jack Regal is the executive director, an imposing, bullish-looking man with a strong, pockmarked face, a dominant nose, and curly brown hair. He has a commanding presence: when he says something, you better believe it. He is trying to change Homewood Terrace from an orphanage to a treatment institution. There are three trained social workers on the staff now and a psychiatrist, Max Silver. They have weekly counseling sessions with the kids.

Jack; his wife, Edna; and daughter, Jill, live in the director's cottage near the administration building. Edna is a quiet, soft-spoken woman who worships her husband. Jill, a chubby twelve-year-old, looks like her dad. They often invite us to their house for work-play social evenings. Jack pours generous drinks of bourbon, and Edna is famous for her delicious roast beef dinners. Jill is usually playing with friends in an adjacent room. The other night she had Brigitte over, one of the kids in cottage 28. The evening ended with the girls having an argument. Brigitte was sent home. Jill said she got mad because Brigitte said bad things about Jill's parents.

The other amazing and noteworthy person in our lives is Hilda Weil, the on-site manager. Born and raised in Germany, she has red hair and is less than five feet tall. She is a fireball, present everywhere, noticing the smallest nuance. When we arrived, she even had a stuffed toy in Danny's crib. He was only eight months old then and liked the teddy. Hilda also stocked our refrigerator for our arrival: fresh tomatoes and a juicy steak, as well as bread, milk, and coffee.

I take Danny for walks in his stroller on Ocean Avenue. Amazingly, when we arrived in August, we dressed Danny in his snowsuit from Racine. August is a very foggy month and cold in the Sunset District.

Nyunyu takes the K streetcar to her new job, at Powell and Market. She got a job at the Woolworth store, baking pizza for take-out customers. Each slice costs twenty-one cents. Nyunyu makes fifty cents an hour, almost $30 a week with occasional tips. Nyunyu volunteered to help out at the infirmary here at the Home on Sundays. There are always kids who come in with cuts and bruises.

There is a pediatrician on call, Dr. Seymour Zoger, a nice man. We have taken Danny to see him in his office for periodic checkups. Dr. Zoger treats babies gently.

Home Again
May 10, 1963

I unfastened my seatbelt. My plane was landing at the Ferihegy Airport in Budapest. I was returning to my native city after fifteen years abroad. I had left during the Stalin regime, when passports were denied to students. In the 1950s, every young person was supposed to stay home and build the Communist regime. But now, with the "thaw" between East and West, tourists were encouraged to come and see the wonders of the socialist system, rebuilding the welfare state, where everyone was equal. I was only thinking of my dad—from whom I had parted so sadly, not knowing whether we would ever be reunited—and my paternal aunt Klára, whom I had missed during my long years in the United States. How would our reunion be?

Before I could gather my thoughts it was time to line up at the immigration queue, foreigners in one line, Hungarian passports to the left. A brusque, heavyset woman with dark-rimmed glasses asked me, "How much foreign currency did you bring with you? Only $100 is permitted per person. Do you have any gold, diamonds, or jewelry to declare?"

Prepared for the questions, I answered, "I have $100 only, and my wedding ring is all I have to declare."

The brusque immigration officer affixed three stamps in my passport and moved me on. After retrieving my heavy suitcase—I had brought warm clothing, chocolates, and cosmetics for all my relatives—I exited through the magic doors that separated the travelers from the locals. I was in the arms of my dad and aunt within seconds, in a long, long embrace.

"You look taller now!" said Dad.

"Your raincoat and shoes look so American," said my aunt. "Did you have a good trip? Welcome home! We were counting the days till your return!"

We were all so happy to be together again! I wiped a tear. These fifteen years had aged Dad. He now walked with a stoop. And Aunt Klára was so thin! In her big overcoat she looked like a frail bird. But I hid these sad thoughts from my loved ones. I called my dad "Apu," as I had when a child.

"Apuka! Tell me how your new job is working out," I asked. My dad had had to leave the bank and now was a bookkeeper at the nationalized Kodak factory, called Forte.

"Well, you know I have to commute to Vac, to the factory. The train ride takes two hours and it's cold in those trains in the winter. The people I work with are all young, mostly party officials, and we all must conform to party politics, which is only right." He winked at me here. "My colleagues all respect me, the old timer. I earn enough to support my modest needs." He sighed, "Your Aunt Klára lives on a small pension. She often has no money left by the middle of the month, but we help each other out. She makes Sunday meals for me and I buy her groceries. We are poor, but proud people still, and we manage within our means."

By then the taxi had pulled up at the hotel. I explained, "My room has been reserved and paid for in the United States so that the Hungarian government would receive the pre-set rate in dollars. I paid $100 for a single room at the Gellert Hotel and I paid $50 daily for expenses. My meals are all taken care of."

At the desk, the concierge said, "Hungarian relatives are not permitted in the hotel rooms." Crestfallen, we had to say goodbye to each other in the lobby. So we made plans to meet the next day in the coffee shop to share the prepaid luxuries. I went to my room and looked out the window to watch my dad with stooped shoulders walking slowly across the busy road, his arms helping his sister, stepping gently and carefully across the streetcar tracks. They turned around, looked up towards the windows, and waved with big smiles. Their girl was home again.

North Beach, 1964

We loved to explore North Beach in the evenings. The time was 1964 and the Coexistence Bagel Shop was crowded with hip and not-so-hip men and women. Someone was reading poetry at a table, and four people were loudly arguing about the Viet Nam conflict.

"We should stay home and help our own folks," rose the squeaky voice above the others. Shike and I left the hubbub and walked down Grant Street. All the shops were open.

At one shop, candles were glowing in the windows and soft music wafted through the door; it could have been Mozart, a very calm and pleasant place. It was an art gallery called The Scene. We walked in. An older man in a panama hat and a large, well-waxed moustache greeted us.

"Come right in. I am Avrum Rubenstein, and I am a painter. I used to be a math teacher but I gave that up. I am free now to paint, sit by the beach, or just drink wine and talk to my customers. Look around and tell me what you think."

We liked his work. Some of his paintings showed forests and trees, gnarled and lonely. Other paintings featured jazz musicians, animated and transfixed in their music.

Shike said, "What we really would like is a painting that would fit over our fireplace, kind of oblong and not too large."

Avrum searched and moved stacks of canvases in his back room. He showed us portraits of his wife, a lovely woman, and groups of children at play. We felt drawn to his visions of beauty and the moments he captured. The size was not right, however—the paintings were too large or too small.

"What a foolish thing," we thought. "You can't buy a work of art with a yardstick."

Then propped in a dusty corner we found our work of art: horses racing on a racetrack, lots of movement, vivid colors. The horses looked alive.

"Thirty-five dollars," he said.

Not a Raoul Dufy, but an original Avrum Rubenstein. We still have it hanging over the fireplace.

A Snapshot

Here is an old snapshot in my photo album. Sárika is looking out a train window, smiling and waving goodbye to friends, looking as if she will soon burst into tears. In her early sixties, she looks pretty in her summer dress. It is 1968. This was her first visit back to Budapest, after eleven years away from Hungary. She is now leaving for Wien, Austria, to fly back to San Francisco.

This had been a bittersweet visit. Many of her friends were still there to embrace her return, women she had worked with in the scarf-painting cooperative—Edith, Erzsike, Manyi. They were still producing fashionable silk scarves for export to Western countries and they had new stories to share. Her sister-in-law, Klára, came to visit her every morning to have coffee and to talk about years gone by, when their kids were little. She visited the cemeteries and laid flowers on her parents' grave. She remembered them for their good deeds.

She went back to the old vineyard of her father (my grandfather), now inhabited by new owners. The big house where she had spent summers had been divided into three dwellings. The long shady terrace where her family had breakfast was covered now and used as a bedroom for a family with many children who had moved in recently. The open courtyard where once horses pulled up with a stylish carriage was now a vegetable garden through which a small path led to the well. The well had the initials of her father, Szlovák Móricz, in bas relief, *SzM*, the initials now fading in the plaster of the well's side panel. Weeds were popping up all around. The wine cellar was partially demolished. Its former elegant wooden entry door had been torn down, replaced by an aluminum one. The wine barrels were still there, with someone else's vintage ripening into the new "Szomorodni," the local blend of red table wine.

She was nostalgic and sad to leave all this behind, to return to her new life in the United States, in San Francisco. Her life is busy now. She works from 8 a.m. to 4 p.m. as an order-filler in a dress factory. She takes a streetcar to work and back. At work she sorts dresses and pulls them from the finishing department to the shipping station. She lives with her daughter and her family and has three grandsons who need her and who wait for her return. On weekends she bakes cookies, cooks big pots of soup, and babysits. She loves to tell her grandsons stories about the old country, when she had a cook and a cleaning woman, when she did not have to chop onions or wash pots and pans. She used to be the lady of the manor. Things are different now. She has to adjust to the new rules of the new world.

But there is Sunday to look forward to, when she puts on one of her nice dresses, wears her pearls, and dabs perfume behind her ears. Then she is a lady for the day. She meets her Hungarian friends, who came to the United States when she did, and they exchange stories about old and new events in their native tongue. Even the coffee tastes better when the rhythm of the patter is so familiar. It is still music to her ears. Then the photos of the grandchildren come out of the purses and each tells the other that their grandchildren are the best, smartest, most good-looking…almost like in the old country.

As the train pulls away from the Budapest station, Sárika realizes that she has left the past. She is fully in the present now and has no regrets.

This is the Story of Rudi

He was born in Nemesgulács, near Lake Balaton, in 1928. His parents, the Spitzers, ran the general store in the village. They were devout Jews and respected members of the town.

Nemesgulács was on a thoroughfare off the main highway from Budapest to the rural commercial town of Tapolca, the trade center for the local farmers and cattle dealers. Nemesgulács consisted of a main street, a church, a school, a parsonage where the priest lived, and a tavern where locals socialized. The village was proud of its natural mineral well. The residents worked the fields, mostly as tenant farmers. There was a shoemaker, a blacksmith, and a midwife at the end of town who delivered babies, cured colds, and bandaged cuts and bruises. For more complicated problems the people in town either saddled the horses or got on their bicycles to go to Tapolca.

Rudi Spitzer was a mischievous boy. He and his cohorts were apt to use slingshots and often did damage to innocent birds, even cats, on the river bank that surrounded the Spitzer's spacious backyard. The backyard was not for show or for leisurely gatherings. It was a kind of animal pen, where cattle and sheep were brought in before slaughter, a waiting room.

Well, Rudi and his friend Zoli (my father's namesake) were very curious about what was going on and they perched on the elderberry tree to watch the animals being led in. They climbed to the top for a panoramic view. Just as they got comfortable, the big branch they had picked for their seat broke off and split the tree in half. They landed with a thud on the fancy stonework on top of the wine cellar. Rudi cut his head on the back of his scalp as he landed. His wound was bleeding fiercely, while Zoli made it with some scratches on his knees.

Mrs. Spitzer, a jovial, round-faced woman in her fifties, grabbed all the towels and torn-up sheets she could find in the closet to wrap around Rudi's bleeding head wound. Rudi, who was nine, was a strong, robust lad. He could not be handled easily. He flailed his arms to keep his mother away. *"Nem, nem,"* he kept saying. "Don't touch me."

"So much blood," thought Mamma Spitzer. "The boy is going to bleed to death. What to do?" She thought of the midwife and dispatched her trusted maid, Emmi, to fetch Marika, the midwife, to fix up Rudi's cuts. To quiet Rudi, she gave him a good shot of *palinka,* a homemade brandy. Rudi stopped flailing his arms and immediately, peacefully, closed his eyes. The brandy really worked magic.

Rudi fell into a dream. A beautiful golden-haired maiden came and rinsed his bleeding scalp with an elixir of perfume so delicious that he inhaled its fragrance. The maiden's hands were gentle but decisive and his pain vanished in minutes. Then the maiden kissed him on his mouth. Honey sweet lips touched his own. Then the lips moved to his eyes. This was a moment he wanted to hold on to forever. No, he didn't want to wake up. This must be heaven. But his eyes fluttered and opened. Leaning over him were his mother and the maid, Emmi. His mother's voice was gentle but firm. "You can open your eyes, you naughty boy. The midwife closed your wound with a clamp. You will be good as new in a couple days. But no more climbing on the elderberry tree for you! We will have to cut it down. Your accident caused it to break apart. Next year you can work as an apprentice, cleaning out the stables. Your strong arms are ready to do man's work now, instead of aiming slingshots at innocent animals. You will be among the hired help, using up your energy. The midwife's visit cost me two plump hens, and that's 100 *pengo* from the household budget."

Drifting Off: A Dream
While in the Hospital in Melk, Austria
June 1998

She was taken by ambulance to the hospital. That night her breathing had become labored. She was unable to catch her breath. The ambulance attendants asked her if she had asthma. She shook her head no. The oxygen and the cortisone shot helped her feel better again and she took deep lungfuls from the black rubber mask that was placed over her face. The IV solution made her sleepy, and she drifted off into a wonderful dream.

She was in San Gimignano, a hilltown of Italy. She was on the top floor of a palatial home, and as she looked out the window she could see the tiled rooftops of the homes. The tall spires of the church towers beckoned. It seemed that she could see the whole village from her vantage point. At the center of the village she saw people gathered around the fountain. There were vendors and a flower market with colorful bouquets. The church bells began to chime, and she reminded herself that it must be Sunday morning. She had a sense of wellbeing and felt comfortable looking at this scene.

The church door opened and a procession of children emerged. She tried to look at their faces. She noticed that the little girls looked very familiar. They were not the village people but her classmates from her school back home. There was Katie and Annie and Márta. She noticed Eva with her brown braids and Julia with her blonde curls. They were laughing as they skipped along.

The girls were followed by a priest holding up a wooden crucifix. As he was walking to the square she saw, as she looked at it more closely, that the crucifix had become a pole with a Star of David. People were waving banners. It was not the Italian red, white, and green flag but the blue and white colors of Israel.

In her dream the scene had changed to an Israeli village and the townspeople were carrying fruit on biers over outstretched poles—big bunches of ripe grapes, peaches, and pears—a harvest festival. Songs were sung and guitar players followed the farmers. People started to dance at the square.

She decided to go down and join the happy crowds. Her room was getting too hot. She needed air. She wanted to run down to join the people.

At the foot of her bed, as she opened her eyes, a nurse was taking her temperature. The oxygen mask needed to be replaced and the IV was dripping slowly into her arm. She woke up with a smile on her face. She somehow felt that everything would soon be all right. She only needed some rest now.

Panni Plans to Visit Hungary

My sister, Panni, decided to take a trip back to Hungary after fifty years. She had left her native country when she was thirteen and hadn't returned since. I, four years older, with happier pre-war memories, had gone back many times.

Panni had repressed her memory of those bad times. Her childhood had been disturbed during those war-torn years with late night trips to the bomb shelter, when bombs fell and eventually ruined our home. In the winter of the last year of the war, we had little heat, food, and water in the little room we were forced to live in. We huddled around a wood-burning stove whose smoke seared our eyes. She still remembered the pungent, unpleasant smell of pea soup cooking on the stove. We shared the memory of ever-cold, ever-wet feet, resulting from the holes in our shoes and the seemingly incessant rain and snow.

Panni and her husband had been retired for several years and had a harmonious, structured life in Southern California, not far from the homes of their three children. She now had a computer class on Mondays and an art appreciation class on Tuesdays. On Wednesdays she and her husband played golf, and on Thursdays they babysat. They had happy hour at 6 p.m. and dinner at 7. There was comfort in the predictable, and not much was left to chance. Panni had worked hard to achieve that balanced, comfortable life. It would be difficult to upset this harmony by going into the past.

At last curiosity won. She had tried to remember with me the park where we had played hide-and-seek. Another time she spoke of our school, where she had sat with other girls wearing white aprons over their dresses and braided hair with white bows tied at the ends, among neat rows of desks. Then she remembered hobbling, as we learned to skate on the tennis court that became a skating rink in winter.

And she wondered, is the Danube really as wide as she remembered it? Do any neighbors remain in the flats around our old building? Or have some grandkids moved in? And is the bakery still around the corner?

Panni asked me to join her on a trip to our mutual past. I was very excited. I had already gone back a number of times. If we went back together, not only could we explore our happier past but she could move on to the colorful changes of recent years. Almost all of the buildings had been repaired, many repainted in pleasant pastels. The streets were paved. The streetcar tracks were slick and modern. There were no air-raid shelter signs on cellar doors. Young people could not be distinguished from the many German tourists or Italian visitors in blue jeans (called "farmer pants" there) and T-shirts with Nike logos. Hungary, especially Budapest, had embraced the Western World. Panni's dreadful memories might be overcome.

A Letter to My Son
September 12, 2001

My Dearest Raul,

How hard it is to put my thoughts together for you, who are in New York City, there where destruction and horror is still a reality. Yesterday marked the end of innocence and trust in America. We were attacked in a heinous way—unprotected and unprepared—from behind our backs. People died while sitting in an airplane, going home, or visiting a loved one. Young stockbrokers studying the charts of companies to be recommended to their clients, others on the phone, drinking coffee, looking out the window, were shocked to see the unbelievable sight of a jet disappearing into the World Trade Center Tower Two, while the other tower was already collapsing into itself. We heard heroic tales of people jumping out of windows holding hands, running, stumbling down many flights of smoky stairs, helping others, people pulling together in this common plight, running for their lives.

Your own wife was caught up in all this. Cool-headed and brave as ever, she ran above ground when she heard what she thought was a blast and exited the subway at the Wall Street station only to see the dust and debris fly into the air, covering her head to toe. The fumes made it hard to breathe. Luckily, she was wearing a scarf and covered her mouth and nose with it. She stumbled as she ran and had to leave her clogs behind to move faster. She met a young woman crying and sobbing, uncontrollably—she had left her friend behind and worried for her safety amid the flying metal debris. It was as if the end of the world had fallen from the skies upon the crowds of workers in New York.

The visions of this nightmare are still with us. We will never erase these from our communal minds. And life must go on. We cannot let the forces of hatred destroy what is left of New York, our civilization, our community. We join forces and pull together more than ever. We have to share our strength as we share our blood supply. We must pass the cup of water, the shovel to dig, the flashlight to see the light from the darkened tunnel.

Love, from your mother.

Showing My Granddaughter
My Childhood Home
June 15, 2003

Well, Julia, here we are! I am so happy you could travel with me and that I can now show you the house where I grew up. This is an apartment house where many families live. When we lived here families didn't speak much to each other. Mostly, we would greet each other in the elevator or when opening the front door, which we kept locked to discourage strangers. We will go up on the elevator to the fourth floor, where our family lived: my mother, whom you remember as Nyunyu; my father, whom you never met; my sister, Panni; and I. You last saw my sister at my birthday celebration. She was very young when we lived here.

Look at the front door of our old apartment. Someone has put up a "Welcome" sign! I've never met them but they must have heard we were coming to visit. Now another family cooks in the kitchen, looks out the windows at the flowing Danube River and sees the Margaret Bridge lit up at night. A new family sleeps in the beds in the same corners where we once curled up to rest and dream. I used to dream of going to America and seeing the world. I wanted to cross the ocean, to see other lands, to speak with other people in their own languages.

I was sixteen when, one day, my parents packed my sister's and my bags with warm sweaters and scarves, with extra shoes, socks and underwear, with food for the trip, and a watch. We were to cross the border to be free in another land, free to go to school, to the synagogue, and to speak our thoughts, all forbidden in this country at that time. We had to keep secrets even from our friends. My dad, Apu, took us to the train station. We said goodbye and the train took off to the edge of the country, the border. My sister, Panni, and I were very sad. We loved our parents. We were such a close, good family. But our parents could not come because it would attract unwanted attention for a whole family to travel to a border town together on the train. So we were to go ahead and then later they would come after us to meet in that safe city on the other side of the border, in Austria, where people were free. We kissed, hugged, cried, and tried to be brave. My father gave us a blessing, placing his hands on our heads.

"Go in peace and safety. May God guide you on your way," he said. We were always going to think of each other even though we would not be together for a while, a long while maybe. None of us knew how long it would be.

It was many years ago, but now I have returned and I can show you the place that used to be home.

A Long-Anticipated Reunion
May 3, 2006

We had become family friends while Shlomo was doing research in San Francisco, and we'd maintained our friendship with him and his family through correspondence. They had been romantic figures to us, and now, after many years, we would see them in their home.

It was 3 a.m. when our plane landed near Tel Aviv at the Ben Gurion Airport. A man held high a sign with our name on it, then helped us with our big suitcases to his limo. The air was balmy, even humid, although it was the middle of the night. Tired but excitedly awake we stared at the misty scenery as we drove to Jerusalem. The road signs in Hebrew, Arabic, and English had names that reached into the recesses of our memories. The views were wide at first but then narrowed as the road twisted among hills and forests. In an hour we were at our spacious, well-appointed hotel. We touched the mezuzah on the door and fell into bed and into a deep slumber.

A bright sun woke us, and we could see the garden outside our windows with bougainvilleas and calla lilies in glorious bloom. The hotel lobby was above our floor and from it we could see vast vistas, including the Old City walls and gates. We phoned our friends, Nurit and Shlomo, and made plans for the night.

At 7 p.m. sharp a limousine pulled up as we sat in the lobby, and a blonde fashion plate in a red leather coat stepped out. Nurith!

"I don't drive anymore. It's cheaper to hire a taxi," she

explained. "Shlomo is waiting at home. He just had knee surgery and must still take it easy."

The limo took us to the outskirts, to a high-rise apartment complex, where we took an elevator to the sixth floor. To our continuing surprise, another panoramic vista awaited us. The apartment was majestically furnished, with flowers in every vase, beautiful paintings on the walls, and Persian carpets on well-polished parquet floors. Antique cabinets displayed collections of precious glass pieces; Lalique, Baccarat, and Steuben vases sparkled. The table was set with hand-cut crystal wine glasses, cheese platters, and pastry assortments.

Shlomo was resting on the couch, his leg propped up on a pillow. We went to hug him as he smiled and he hugged us back warmly.

"Sorry that I am indisposed but I had to have my knee repaired. I could no longer walk or even stand on it. It will heal in a few weeks. "

Though Shlomo's face was deeply furrowed, showing his concerns, his aura of love and caring made him glow. At seventy-six he still practiced medicine, mostly consulting for the seriously ill.

After toasting our getting together after three long decades and after many joyous comparing of notes, the conversation turned serious, to the Israeli-Arab conflict.

Shlomo stated there is no peaceful solution with terrorists who are bent on destroying you and your children. He is a hawk now and feels that Israel can only survive by showing its military strength. This should be shown on the Lebanese border as well as in Gaza, Shlomo said. He was very bitter and pessimistic about the survival of the Jewish state, with the Arabs multiplying at an alarming rate. We must fight them on all fronts, he argued, including encouraging Israelis to abandon birth control measures and resettling Ethiopians and Russians into Eretz Israel.

Then the conversation turned to Nurit and how she spends her time.

"Of course I help out with my grandchildren, but they are growing up, so there is less need for my babysitting. Nowadays I spend my days at the hairdresser, manicurist, and masseuse. I decided to become a hedonist. I buy fashionable clothes and have lunch with my lady friends. I have done my share of saving the world. The world is going to the dogs anyway. My motto now is *carpe diem*, "seize the day.""

We were very fond of them in San Francisco and even fonder of them in Israel. Yet, somehow, the world had changed in between.

In Memoriam: Zoltán Biró
Father's Day, 2006

I call him "Apu."

Zoli was born Hochstadter Zoltán on December 12, 1891, in Tapolcá, Hungary. Tapolcá is a market town and the county seat of Zala, a province in western Hungary, an area called Dunántúl (beyond the Danube). The town is near the tip of Lake Balaton, in a fertile winegrowing country, a favored vacation area of the locals.

Zoli's parents, Ignácz and Lotte Hochstadter, were comfortably middle-class citizens. Ignácz managed a large agricultural estate and hired help for the fields and horse stables. The land was tilled by horses, and transportation was also provided by horse-drawn carriages. Lotte, a small and frail woman, was in charge of the household and the education of the children. Zoli had two sisters, Rózsa, who was two years older, and Klára, two years his junior. The three attended local schools and were considered bright (though this was at first questioned for Klára, until it was found that poor eyesight had been holding her back). When Zoli reached high school, the family moved to Budapest to provide him with a better education. By the time Zoli received his baccalaureate, the family had changed its family name to Biró, a popular Hungarian name meaning "judge," so that Zoli would matriculate with that Hungarian-sounding and easily pronounced name.

Zoli was a decorated cavalry officer in the First World War. Later he told of cold nights in the field when he slept with his cap on, for which he blamed his hair loss. After the war he enrolled in the Kereskedelmi Akadémia, comparable to a college-level business school here. He got a job as a cashier in the Credit Bank and his career started to move forward. He rented a bachelor apartment in the inner city and, with his earnings, he feathered his nest with nice paintings, Persian rugs, and elegant furniture.

In 1924 Zoli was introduced to Sári Szlovák, the attractive daughter of a nearby vintner. Both families spent summer vacations near Lake Balaton and socialized at generously laden luncheons under the walnut trees. Sári and Zoli married June 21, 1925, at the Bristol Hotel in Budapest. The family was then in mourning. Zoli's father, Ignácz, a robust, florid-faced, cigar-smoking country squire, had suddenly passed away, most likely from a heart attack. Zoli and Sárika set up housekeeping in an elegant apartment at Fö utca II on the Buda side of the Danube quay. The building was owned by Gróf Zichy, and the newlyweds rented one floor. It was furnished in the contemporary art deco style, with baroque touches in the bedroom. A lovely ceramic fireplace graced a corner. The room was surrounded by paintings, cornices, and candelabras.

I was born seven years later, in 1932, and their second daughter, Anna Mária, arrived in 1936. By then war fever was raging in Europe and the Birós started to fear for their lives. War was coming closer. Another change in the family's life occurred when Sári's parents moved in with them, into a large double flat in Zrinyi utca. The household enlarged even more; three servants helped run matters smoothly—a cook, a cleaning woman, and a nanny for the girls. Zoli's mother died in 1939. She suffered from breast cancer and was already an invalid when she was run down by a vegetable vendor's cart.

Sári, Zoli, and family remained close to Zoli's two sisters, Rózsa and Klára, who lived in their new, modern villa on Rózsadomb (Rose hill). The sisters had married two brothers, Paul and Sándor Oblath. Sunday family dinners were always beautifully served and enjoyed by all. A bachelor uncle was invited as well, Hajós Pál, who had the rank of nobility *(méltó ságos)*. The whole Oblath-Biró family had an air of gentility and elegance. Nonetheless they were most loving and kind with me and my sister. Sári worshipped her sisters-in-law. They respected each other.

I now fast-forward our family history to 1940 and describe how our life was at that time.

Zoli Biró and family live at Klotild utca 3/b now, a spacious, fourth-floor apartment. Sári's mother, Aranka, has had a heart attack and is under nursing care twenty-four hours a day. She gets oxygen from large tanks, delivered regularly and administered by a live-in nurse. The doctor visits regularly and keeps Aranka's health stable. Zoli is now president of the Credit Bank's "Berlin Place" office *(Berlini térfiók)*. He dresses sharply and cuts a handsome figure. He gets manicures and splashes eau de cologne on his clean-shaven face. He walks Ági to school daily and they chat in rhythm with their brisk steps. He has to be on time and teaches the girls the virtue of punctuality. Grandmother Aranka Szlovák dies after a bout of pneumonia on September 21, 1941. Grandfather Morris Szlóvak remains with the family. He regularly takes the train to the vineyard in Badacsony and remains vigorous into his late seventies.

German dominance over Hungarian politics is intensified. German forces occupy Hungary on March 19, 1944, and take complete control over the fate of its citizens. All military-age men who are not in the army have to join forced labor battalions. Zoli is fifty-three and is assigned to a demolition road repair unit in Csepel, a river island south of Budapest, where major factories and warehouses are located. Allied bombings are frequent. Factories are targeted. Zoli's labor force job has become dangerous. He and his and crew have to defuse unexploded bombs and clear rubble. He sends postcards to his family to reassure them that he is still alive and well. Thankfully he is not shipped out of the country.

In December 1944 the family takes shelter in Zugló with false papers, moving into the apartment of an AWOL Hungarian soldier. Zoli's colleague and friend, Géza Méhes, finds this safe house. Zoli bribes one of his guards at the forced labor battalion *(Munkaszolgalat)* with a gold coin sewn into the hem of his trousers, and makes him swear on the life of his child that he will not reveal the address of our hiding place. Zoli joins his family, taking shelter from the bombs in the coal cellar.

The siege of Budapest, between Russian attackers and German defenders, is in full force. This war is severe and cruel, and to stay alive is a matter of luck. Budapest has been cut off from all food supplies. Stores are shuttered. Water mains freeze. People melt snow to drink. There is no heat or fuel. The Birós bundle up with layers of clothing in their coal-cellar hideaway. They eat dry bread and use well-hidden bacon to survive. They are liberated by the Russian troops on January 8, 1945. The family has survived the siege and the war.

Towards the end of January 1945, Zoli and his brother-in-law Béla, Sári's older brother who has joined the family's shelter, venture out to see if the old apartment house is still standing. They hope to move back home now that the Germans are defeated. Zoli and Béla travel on foot, hiding in doorways, stepping over corpses, and avoiding marauding, pilfering Russian soldiers. They walk some twenty kilometers to the center of town where the Danube is, and find the Klotild utca apartment house in ruins. A bomb has hit the inside of the courtyard and the top three floors have collapsed into each other. The residents of the building were living in the shelter on the first floor of the building, where empty offices were still intact.

Zoli, Sári, Grandfather, Béla, Ági, Panni, and by now two Oblath nephews pile their earthly belongings—clothes, food items, pots and pans—on a hand-pulled cart and make their way through the boulevards to their old home. There are stray bullet shots. The Germans are entrenched on the Buda side of the city, across the Danube. The cart gets too heavy. The family is weak from hunger. Sári finds a horse and cart along the boulevard, she buys the horse, and they pile their stuff on this cart. When they arrive at Klotild utca, fierce fighting erupts from the Germans, who must think that Russian forces are in the street. The horse is shot down and dies. Neighbors note that the horse has been carved up for meat within hours. The family struggles with the luggage, to pull it into safety. The Birós set up housekeeping in an office space. Their luggage becomes their bed. They locate a stove for roasting chestnuts and use it for cooking, venting it out the windows.

Zoli's first trip takes him to the bank where he works, at the end of the street. He finds it in flames, burning on the inside. He does not hesitate. He goes in and rescues some important documents from the safe.

Life slowly returns to normal. Some trains resume service. Peasants bring food items to the city. Informal bartering markets are set up along the boulevards: a live chicken for a set of bed linens; a sack of potatoes for a pair of men's shoes. The war ends in June. Grandfather and Zoli climb on board an overcrowded passenger train to see how the vineyards fared during the war and to reestablish their claim to their old estate.

After several days of traveling they reach their old estate and find the caretaker, Virág, who had been in service for twenty years. Virág welcomes them and later tells the story of watching two starving "beggars" come up the road, who turned out to be my father and grandfather. After their welcome, each consumes six eggs, a whole loaf of bread, and a liter of milk. Zoli and Grandfather find the cellar ransacked, the wine barrels empty but the framework still intact. The grapevines are still in place but the house has been torn down by the locals, brick by brick.

Zoli eventually returns to the bank, gets a promotion for his bravery, and slowly life returns to normal. The family moves to the intact building next door. They pull whatever furniture remains from the old home across the bombed out rubble to a new, smaller apartment. For the Birós, 1945 to 1948 are years of change. The girls, Ági and Panni, are back to school. Zoli works. Grandfather spends much of his time at the vineyard.

On October 31, 1949, Zoli takes his two daughters, Ági and Panni, to the train station and says good-bye to them. They are going to cross the border to Austria and find a new, freer life in the United States with Uncle Andy and Aunt Sylvia. The Biró family splits up, and Zoli and Sári are now on their own.

Zoli suffers a heart attack and dies on December 13, 1963, at his home, the morning after his seventy-second birthday. His legacy and memory live on in his family in the United States.

Epilogue

Is there anything I left out of Zoli's life story? Nothing purposefully, but some details could be added. What would I like to mention now?

To tell more about my relationship to my father, Zoli Biró.

I loved my father. He was a good father. He was not a chummy, hands-on, sit-in-my-lap kind of father. We were friends and confidants. I listened to his wisdom—about politics, world events, how the universe functioned. I opened the door for him when I heard his footsteps, when he came home for his noonday meal. I kibitzed with him after he finished his meal. I helped him with "noise diversions" when he turned on the radio to listen to the Voice of America, after the war. He listened to the BBC nightly, even when it was forbidden by the socialist government.

My father, Zoli, suffered his first heart attack when I was reunited with him after fourteen years' absence. I was back in

Budapest for the first time. He went to the bank to meet his new boss, and that is when he became faint and fell ill. It was not until days afterwards that an EKG diagnosed the heart attack. After two weeks I had to say goodbye to him while he was still in the hospital. This was a very heart-wrenching experience for me. I feel he died too soon. We still had a lot to say to each other. I learned then not to postpone doing things with people. Do it at the moment and don't wait for future opportunities. They may never come.

Remembering Nyunyu
February 16, 2007

I picked a flower today. It was a daisy and I brought it to my Mother's grave. Maybe it will bloom and tell the world that she is not forgotten. She never will be, while I am alive, while my sons are here, and my granddaughter is dancing and singing.

We are the witnesses of her rich life—almost a century of teaching us and others about the traditions of our culture and the beauty of our Jewish heritage, the secrets of Hungarian cuisine, and the ins and outs of a loving family and keeping a happy home together.

She brought us good cheer and taught us diplomacy. She knew how to adapt to a new world, to adopt a new country, and to learn a new language, again and again.

We light a candle for you, Nyunyu.

Four Days of Bliss
May 1, 2007

We had planned the trip to New York for months. This was to be a special family gathering: our son's wedding to sweet Jennifer.

For weeks we prepared our festive clothing. Shike was fitted for a tuxedo. I went to a bridal shop and found a silvery, shimmering evening dress. I rummaged through my jewelry box for sparkling accessories. Shike asked his other two sons to lend him cufflinks to wear with the pleated shirt. Suitcases were readied, bridal gifts ordered, airplane tickets purchased, hotel rooms reserved. The big day for the departure arrived. We got to the airport early and no, there were no delays in the plane's departure. It was on time. We got our aisle seats and even ordered the box lunch for $5 with a glass of Chablis to wash it down. The six hours in the air flew by. We landed at JFK and stepped into the limo waiting for us. The air was balmy in New York, a pleasant 70 degrees. Our dear son Raul waited for us at the hotel with a colorful bouquet of carnations, my favorite flower.

"Dinner will be at our house tonight. Jennifer has prepared the spread: tofu burgers with cole slaw, all veggie and low cal. You will love it."

Soon we were toasting their health around the table. The next day, we met Jenn's parents, two handsome, youthful people, very eager to see their daughter wed to a principled, even-tempered, talented man, our son. The wedding itself was a dream. The *chuppah* was erected in the ballroom of the hotel: pink and ivory

113

roses formed a garland above it. There were bouquets of the same roses in tall vases around the room.

The music was played by Raul's Hungarian folk musicians. They played old village melodies on their fiddles, with a harp strumming the harmony. The rabbi, a young woman with an Israeli *kippah,* spoke of their deep commitment to each other and their spiritual legacy, the continuation of family traditions and values.

She said, "You can improvise your lifestyle and dress code, but never stint on your religion. In the final count, that is what will keep you going."

Eulogy for My Sister:
Rest in Peace, Panni

Pannika, we are here with you. We gather round you, we miss you. We are here at the old walnut tree where you and I played in the sandbox as children. This was our home away from home, where we grew up with our parents, our grandparents, uncles, and friends, some of whom came from afar to visit, to also find a home away from home and an island of peace.

Then came war. Our childhood, our lives, were shattered. We huddled in bomb cellars, we were hungry, we were cold, we were afraid. Our parents were our shelter and we survived. But where we hoped to return to some kind of normalcy, the new regime brought new restrictions and fears. We fled our walnut tree and our home to another world altogether. Our good relatives took us in, helped us into the university, to new careers. We married, raised families, established homes, and…got older.

You, my dearest Panni, became the mother of a handsome son and two lovely daughters. You had completed an advanced degree and founded a learning center, The Growing Years, a primary school where children could learn in a caring and cheerful environment. You created the framework for this nurturing environment because you knew what was relevant in educating the young. You provided inspiration to your students with the three R's. Several hundred students passed through the portals and went on to successful higher learning centers from your school. Your home bloomed as well. You and your beloved Roger created an oasis in your residence in La Canada. There was even a fishpond on your lower deck. Your three children grew up and flew out of the nest.

Cruel fate did not give you the time to enjoy the fruits of your labor. You fought a brave battle and kept your social graces to the very end. You smiled when getting around and speaking became incredibly difficult. You remained your living, gracious self throughout your battle with the brain tumor. Roger nursed you for ten years and kept your lifestyle at the level that you were used to. The table was set even at the last family dinner, with the Herend china, fresh flowers in a vase, and crystal water goblets.

Your spirit is still here with us. Your inspiring personality continues to live within us. Rest in peace. We love you forever.

Eulogy for My Brother-in-Law, Roger
June 2007

Roger is in my thoughts today. I see his limber athletic walk as he strides down Esplanade Drive. He is going to join his family, his grandkids, for a picnic on the beach. He wears his well-creased, well-worn hat, and is smiling happily when he sees the kids.

"Here comes Grandpa," says Lauren cheerfully. "Now we can have fun."

Roger is Grandpa.

Roger is Dad.

Roger is "Hey Dear" to Panni.

Roger is our brother-in-law.

Roger is Uncle Roger.

Roger is Prince Charming.

Roger is always even tempered, always upbeat, never moody or angry or mean. Roger is calm and collected. You can count on him.

I look back on fifty years of family togetherness. Roger came into our family in 1957 when Panni introduced him to us in Racine, Wisconsin. They had driven from Madison in Roger's 1947 roadster. They seemed happy from the start.

Roger was tall and handsome; quiet, but when he spoke he made us laugh. Golf was his passion, and his life revolved around his game. He grew up on a country-club golf course in Freeport, Illinois. His dad handed him his first clubs when he was knee high. He was loyal to his fraternity.

Panni and Roger were a beautiful couple. They complemented each other in every way.

Their wedding, on June 28, 1958, in Rockford, was a candle-lit, daisy-chained romantic celebration. Roger's parents, Clara and Harry, were glowing. All of their friends attended, and the party went on till all hours. After the wedding, a honeymoon in the Bahamas and then on to the pro circuit. They drove their old car across country, arriving at all the championship playoffs tired and in need of a shower and some rest. Roger and Panni found modest B&Bs. But they ran out of their savings and their winnings in about a year. They happened to be in Los Angeles, where they liked the mild climate, and decided to settle there.

They rented an apartment and started to make it home. Family friends, Hope and Howard, lived nearby and welcomed them to the neighborhood. Soon after, Shike and I moved to San Francisco and were a little closer to them. Panni and Roger, the flexible newlyweds, would drive up to see us for the weekend. We had a baby and were less able to travel. Also Nyunyu, our mother, had arrived by then from Hungary and was living with us. Nyunyu always made festive, delicious meals when Panni and Roger visited, all their favorites: *korozott, palacsinta,* wonderful soups with feather-light dumplings, tortes, and soufflés to make your mouth water and eyes pop in amazement.

I recall Roger saying once, "Nyunyu, you treat me as if I were a king."

Panni got a teaching job. Roger became an insurance adjuster with Lynn T. Hodge, a family-owned insurance brokerage. The newlyweds moved into a home, where they lived for decades, on Lila Lane in La Canada. Stefan arrived in 1965 and Andrea came two years later. Soon, a little sister, Marina, joined her, and the family was complete. The house was enlarged. A family room, large outdoor decks, and a fish pond made the hacienda more unique and spacious. The family added a little dachshund called Bonus and then other doggies joined the fold, until there were five canines barking.

Panni and her friend Sue Bloom created a new school, The

Growing Years, a marvelously administered private school that grew each year, from grades K to 6. They excelled in their curriculum.

Panni and Roger established a wonderful friendship circle. They became gourmet cooks and antiques buffs. They traveled to Hawaii and to their cabin in the Sierras. Panni and Roger took cruises to Alaska, the Caribbean, and to Asia. They traveled to Europe. We had a wonderful, memorable trip to Italy together. We went from Milan to Florence and San Giminiano. Another year it was back to Hungary. One year they invited us on our very first sailing to the Caribbean, a memorable experience. Panni was the ultimate elegant passenger at sea.

The years passed rapidly and soon college graduations and weddings graced the family calendars.

It is so sad that this idyllic life was cut short by Panni's illness, an inoperable brain tumor. She fought bravely for ten years until the end, in 2005, with Roger at her side, keeping the home sparkling, the medical appointments met, and the family intact, with Panni at the head of the table, as always.

After Panni's death, Roger tried to keep going, meeting his golf friends weekly, exercising Pancsur, the vizsla, and spending time with the grandkids. But illness and sadness took their toll. After a year's struggle with a relatively rare medical condition, he was back at Stefan and Anna's home, as he wished, among his family, out of the hospital.

Roger and Panni's memory will be a blessing for all who knew them. May they rest in peace.

A Family Gathering
October 20, 2007

What an amazing weekend we shared. The family gathered from across the country in Madison, Wisconsin, for Katrina's bat mitzvah. The well-remembered progenitors were Katrina's maternal great-grandfather (Elik or Zaideh) and great-grandmother (Bubie), both deceased. Their final home, on Madison Street, was still owned by the family. The great-grandparents' children were: Great-Uncle Shike, married to Aggie, of San Francisco (whose youngest, Raul, came with his wife Jennifer from Brooklyn); Grandfather David and Grandmother Renie, of Madison; lovingly remembered Great-Aunt Anita, deceased; and Uncle Andy, an artist, of Philadelphia. Anita's three children grew up in Madison; the eldest, Aunt Cheryl, now lives in Omaha, and Uncle Murray occupies the Madison Street home. Katrina's mother is Naomi, David and Renie's only child.

"What should we do first?" asked Cheryl. The homestead was the answer, for the first stop. Cousin Murray lives there now with his step-daughter, his dachshund Max, and two cats. The house was newly painted but sparsely furnished. A huge plasma TV was the focal point in front of the fireplace. Great grandfather's study-corner was but a memory. That is where his desk was, with his bookcase behind him, said Cheryl, who used to visit her grandparents often. Grandma's armchair was where the plump leather couch is now. She used to sit there and look out on the street to watch the birds, and the flowers she planted. No, the house is different now, but the old spirit lingers. Then it was time to go to the synagogue, walking distance from the old house, because on the Sabbath, Grandpa Elik would not get into a car but walked, rain or shine.

Temple Beth Israel was bedecked with flowers for Katrina's big day. When the family arrived, she was already reading the Torah portion at the pulpit. She read slowly and steadily, with self-assurance. She smiled as she noticed the arriving guests. At age thirteen she was tall, long hair parted in the middle, wavy brown hair framing her rosy cheeks. She wore a navy blue and white polka dot dress and matching high-heeled shoes, and, on her neck, the shiny gold chain with the Star of David that her grandmother Renie gave her for this special occasion.

Then the family was called up to say their blessings for the young celebrant. Her parents, her uncle, her cousins, all went up and later formed a circle around her, signifying the family sharing the blessed occasion when their young niece became part of the congregation. She is considered an adult. She can lead the congregation if needed, or be called upon to complete a *minyan*. God bless Katrina, the bat mitzvah, and the pride of the family. May she continue to believe and carry on the traditions of generations and the generations before her! She carries the Torah now.

An Imagined Visit to Badacsony

We had planned to carry out my deceased sister Panni's wish that her ashes be placed under the oak tree in Grandfather's vineyard. The plan did not go forward because the vineyard area had become a shambles and because a school schedule conflict prevented my sister's daughter-in-law from coming. So we made and carried out another plan, and her ashes were buried in the Buda hills. But this is how I imagined it originally.

Panni's children, Andrea and Stefan; Stefan's wife, Anna; Panni's friend Ethel; and I would take the train from Budapest to Badacsony, a four-hour trip on the rapid train. We would be in a newer second-class compartment, similar to an American commuter train, with plastic-covered seats, two facing each other, and small racks for weekend bags. We would have packed sandwiches, apples, and cookies so we would need only water when we got to the train. Anna would have made sandwiches in foil—rye bread, cream cheese, slices of red pepper—crunchy and tasty. The cookies would have been baked by my Hungarian friend, Julika, following an old family recipe, with hazelnuts and raisins in pastry dough.

Four hours on the train would have given us lots of time to talk. Perhaps Anna would give more details of her visit to Hong Kong two years ago, when she re-met her real dad, whom she had not seen since she left Burma, twelve years before. Had he changed much? How?

Then I would tell about my grandfather, how he looked when I last saw him at the vineyard we were going to visit, how he had been standing on the platform of the train station waiting for us, leaning on his cane, wearing black boots and a suit that consisted of jodhpurs, vest, and a coat jacket draped over his shoulders, his handlebar moustache waxed. He would have been in his seventies by then but he stood erect, and he moved rapidly to embrace us. At the time I remember him like that, there was just the three of us: my mother, Nyunyu; my sister, Panni, then twelve years old; and I, then sixteen. My grandfather was saying, "The horses and carriage are behind the station house.... Mr. Kovacs will help you with your bags.... Welcome.... I am so glad that you got here safely.... Mrs. Kovacs made a delicious goulash for us, and baked fresh bread too.... The cherries have ripened and I picked a bowlful for your dessert...."

That was how I remembered our first trip to the vineyard after the war and after the siege of Budapest, when it had become safe to travel. Our mother, Nyunyu, was then forty-three years old. Usually full of vitality and energy, she had been worn out by the hardships of war and deprivation. Her once rich brown locks were now tinged with grey. She was wearing my father's shoes, since her feet had suffered frostbite during the cold winters. Short skirts were passé in 1947. She had her dress altered to become fashionably longer by piecing two skirts together to look nice. My sister and I wore hand-knitted sweaters and jumpers and we carried small rucksacks with our precious possessions like our diaries, books to read, flashlights, and small provisions of nuts and raisins, which in Hungary was called "student staple," *diak eledel.* We were looking forward to the visit, remembering our pre-war summers spent with grandfather at the old vineyard, where the living was easy, a memory which shined in the aftermath of the dreadful war.

The train tracks had been bombed. Once we had to get off the train and walk some distance to the connecting train. During the war Grandfather's vineyard had been assigned to a Nazi officer and his family. Grandfather had just completed the legal formalities to reclaim ownership of his old estate. Luckily the tax records were intact and the deed of purchase still on file. He had cleaned out the house, repainted the walls, changed the straw in the mattresses, cleaned and limed the outhouse, and polished and restocked the stove with kindling and firewood. There was plenty of clean water in the well. He had pails filled and ready for our use. There was no electricity or running water in those days in Badacsony. We used kerosene lamps, visited the outhouse, and washed in a wash basin with a pitcher of water handy.

Much of the produce was grown on the farm, like the potatoes and the onions and the parsley for our goulash soup. Flour for the bread came from the wheat taken to the mill and ground for each customer. The meat came from local cattle, slaughtered by the butcher. The caretaker and his wife lived in the cottage next to Grandfather's house. They had been there for decades. They received an annual retainer and used the crops as part of the family. They hired the day workers when the grapes ripened and when the cherries were to be picked. Mrs. Kovacs made preserves from the cherries for winter.

This is how far I got in my story when the conductor came in and announced, "Next stop Badacsony." Time to get off the train.

Fifty years had gone by since I last got off the train. Four Americans and one native would now be coming back to the old country. What will our family adventure of 2008 be like?

Santa Claus Arrives
December 24, 2008

You can't escape the spirit of Christmas. It finds you wherever you are. It found me today in Mazatlan, Mexico. Santa Claus arrived on a golf cart draped in red velvet fabric. He was jolly, fat, and ringing a bell, smiling from ear to ear. Alongside the cart were twelve reindeer—young, healthy girls skipping merrily. Santa gave handfuls of candy to all he passed on his way through the well-tended lawns, to the palapa by the beach, and along the swimming pool, where I was swimming. All the bikini-wearing beauties got a handful of candy, chips, and toys. Santa was generous to all. He made his way back slowly, to the parking lot, and, sleigh bells still ringing, disappeared from sight. There was something naïve and sincere about the whole kitschy event. He had brought the spirit of the day. His bell found an echo in my heart. I had to think of old times, good times, bad times, new times, and long forgotten times, where I encountered him.

Back in childhood—the year could have been 1938, 1939, who knows—a small Christmas tree, candles lit, sat on the grand piano. Nyunyu opened the doors and the magic was there. Back then we were told Christmas trees were for the sake of the servants. We were Jewish. We celebrated Chanukah. But that small pine tree and the light that shone around it stayed in my mind.

Then came 1944, never to be forgotten: we were in Zugló, hiding. There was no Christmas tree, just pine branches at the middle of the table. The presents were toothbrushes that my mother managed to find on a shelf in a drugstore. The meal was a goose that the innkeeper by the railroad track raised in his backyard. We lived off it for weeks. It was cooked in tomato sauce that night. A bomb came whistling down to a neighboring house, hit it, and our windows blew out. There were glass shards everywhere, but we quickly salvaged the meal and wrapped it in kitchen towels in the kitchen. We mused that the tomato sauce could easily have been our blood, but we were lucky this time.

The year is 1950. We are in Rockford now, surrounding the ceiling-high Christmas tree at Andy and Sylvia Slovak's. I recall the glittering gold ornaments, beautifully wrapped gifts under the tree, the table set with beautiful china and silver, Grandmother Sorensen telling us to wear our best dresses tonight. It is Christmas, the best day of the year. Panni and I are all smiles, filled with gratitude at our good fortune that we are in America. Secretly we long for our parents and our grandfather, still in dark, oppressed Communist Hungary. Nyunyu and Apu are just recovering from the horrors of being in prison. How can there be so much glitter and sadness at the same time?

Happy times are here again. It is 1959 now and a lot has changed in our lives. Panni and Roger are married and we all live in California. Nyunyu is out of Hungary, though Apu chose to stay there and live the best he can. His health is not so good after all the hard times. He still has his home and job there now. We are having Christmas in Los Angeles together for the first time. Dan is a baby and we are driving our 1956 Chevrolet. Nyunyu baked Christmas cookies for everyone. She made walnut and poppyseed *beigli*, like in the old days. We pack up the car; enough diapers for the baby and off we go. Life is good and family times are cozy and meaningful again. We are branching out to a new generation. Panni and I both have husbands and homes of our own. There is a lot to celebrate now. Although we still count pennies, there are gifts for all.

Back to the present. Where did the intervening fifty years go, slipping away like a dream? The spirit of love is still here, with me, now, in Mazatlan. Memory is a precious thing. I hope to keep it forever.

The Story of Szlovák Mór
My Grandfather, Nyunyu's Dad

Móricka was born October 13, 1871, in Gyulakeszi, Hungary. His father's name was Ignácz. His mother's name is unknown to me. She died in the flu epidemic of 1917, which decimated the population in Hungary. There were no antibiotics or sulfa back then and young women seemed to have succumbed to it easily.

Village life was simple and structured. Ignácz, his dad, was the village school teacher. He commanded respect but meager pay. The family lived in a house on the main street. My grandfather's cousin Rudi Somogyi pointed it out to me. Gyulakeszi was a town near Tapolca, the county's trading center. The population lived by farming, raising cattle, and producing milk. They supplied the folks in the cities of Tapolca and Keszthely.

Ignácz Szlovák remarried shortly after his wife's death. There were Jewish families in all the nearby villages: the Spiegel family in Káptalan topi and the Grosz family in Badacsony. He married one of the Grosz daughters and moved to Badacsony-tomaj. He bought a nice small house at the edge of town. (I visited the rebuilt house in 2008, with some of my family.) There Ignácz started to raise a new family. Two sons and a daughter were born in rapid succession: Endre, Laci, and Elza. Great-Grandfather had a third wife, and one son, Jozsef, was born from this union. I personally knew Laci the best; he was like an uncle to us. He was a handsome man, and ended up marrying a daughter of the well-known Héber family, the father being a well-to-do vintner in Gyongyos, which is north of Budapest, near Eger. I recall a weekend visit to their affluent yet gracious home when I was five. His wife, Manci, and son, Andras, remain etched into my memory. Alas, the Hébers as well as Laci's family were deported and killed in Auschwitz. A granddaughter, Kati Héber, born in 1947, is alive.

Back to my grandfather: His stepmother also died when Móricz was twelve years old, and they sent him to be an apprentice butcher with the Spitzer (Somogyi) family in Nemesgulács. Móricz lived with his cousin's family and helped slaughter cattle, pigs, and sheep in their backyard, and prepared the meat for sale in the retail butcher shop in front of the general store on the main street. They treated him like a son and he grew up in a hurry. He married at a young age an orphan daughter of a second cousin, Aranka Fenyvesi, who had been visiting in Badacsony for the summer. Aranka grew up at Szentendre, upstream on the Danube, north of Budapest. She was a lovely, intelligent woman who read poetry. She often quoted poems by Petőfi and Arany, contemporary Hungarian writers. It was a very happy, loving marriage.

Móricz had six grades of education, having left home so young. His teacher was the local rabbi, who taught him all the prayers, all the melodies for the Sabbath and high holidays. Our grandfather even knew how to blow the *shofar*. He embraced his Jewish religion as the core of his existence and the guiding light of ethical practices in life.

Aranka and Móricz had two sons: Béla, born in 1897, and Andrew/Andor, born in 1899, as well as a precious daughter, Charlotte, born in 1904. (Charlotte, or Sári, or Sárika, was our mother, "Nyunyu.") Móricz and Aranka moved to Budapest by the time the kids were born. They first lived at Rottenbiller utca 35, near the city park (Város liget). Sárika often talked of going to a little park near Andrassy út—Kodály Korond. She and her mother would pack a lunch and she played ball with other little girls while her older brothers got into boyish mischief on their own. Béla was seven and Andy five when she was born, and by the time she reached kindergarten age they were strong lads. They went to gymnasium already and were very independent.

The summers were spent in Badacsony tomaj, where Móricz acquired a vineyard and built a country house. The place is still named Szlovák Major. He became a practiced vintner, and sold his wine by the barrel. His occupation now was that of a cattle buyer. He went to estates and inspected cattle for purchase by the large slaughterhouses in the city.

My grandfather sported a handlebar moustache, wore boots and jodhpurs. He had baby-blue eyes and a mischievous grin as he looked at us lovingly. He adored his daughter, Nyunyu/Sári, and spoiled his granddaughters, Ági (yours truly) and Panni. He knew how to handle his horses. I never saw him riding a horse, only in his horse-drawn carriage. There were some carriages for work in the fields and others for elegant transport of the family. In the summers, the Szlováks invited their friends for country weekends and swimming or at least bathing in Lake Balaton.

This was now the turn of the twentieth century and Lake Balaton had become a fashionable resort. A train connected the city with the country, and little villas sprung up in the hillsides. Badacsony was—and is—the pearl of the lake.

The Szlováks had their private cabin near the beach, to dress and undress in. Béla and Andor knew how to scare the ladies. They caught some green frogs by the lake and dropped them on the innocent ladies through the vent holes on top of the dressing cabins. These were days of discovery and well being, which all ended with the winds of war of World War I. But that is another story.

My grandfather's final blessing to us as we left our family home in 1949, to cross the borders and travel across oceans, was, "Travel safely, and never forget your faith, your traditions, and your family."

His generous spirit and family commitment have guided me all my life. His final blessing still rings in my ears.

Looking Back Upon My Life

Once I was a young girl. I wore my hair in pigtails, always had a smile on my face, and played with my dolls. And always, I felt my mother's presence. I watched her bake cakes, cook meals, set the table, and talk to her friends on the telephone. I noticed that when she went out, she dressed nicely, wore hats, and put on perfume. I heard her bracelets jangle when she came to my room and kissed me goodnight. My mother was my role model from early on. I was impressed by her homemaking skills and social ease, and came to think she was the smartest person in the world. I learned from and copied her actions. I wanted to be just as nice as she was when I grew up.

The years passed and I noticed that I was becoming a woman. My body now had curves, and I felt good when I dressed up and people noticed me on the street. I fell in love with a handsome, dark-haired boy. We kissed, held hands, and walked in the park. The future seemed rosy, yet bewildering. I wanted to go to college and see the world. My life seemed too narrow at home. I wanted to travel and experience new things. I did not want to be tied down just yet. There was a conflict in self-realization goals between following in my mother's well-formed social structure and creating a life of independence.

Before long, I found myself across the oceans, in a new world where people spoke a strange and foreign language. They ate foods unfamiliar to me, drove big cars, and their speech seemed filled with platitudes. I felt lonely and longed for my old home, childhood family, and old lifestyle. I was displaced and alienated. I was in the out-group now. I did not belong to the customs and mores of my adopted land.

But once again, I observed my peers and listened to my teachers. After college I found a job helping children who had no homes and needed placement. People listened to me and followed my advice. I married a good man. We understood each other and were on the same emotional wavelength. We started our own family. My three sons thought their mommy was smart and knew how to bake bread and serve soup. I bandaged their bruises and tucked them in at night. I became a full-time homemaker and found it challenging to become a role model myself. I was an honest and loving mother. They grew up and left our home. The nest became empty. I adjusted to the shift in generations and my own middle age gradually.

My mother grew older and needed a helping hand every now and then. The decades passed and she turned seventy, then eighty. But she remained young at heart. She was always ready to go to various cultural institutions and concerts, and sometimes volunteer there. She mended her grandsons' torn blue jeans and, yes, she still baked her wonderful cakes. She showed me how to get older graciously and to stay young at heart forever. My mother's age helped me realize that there are satisfactions as well as challenges at every age.

As I review my life, I see that I was never excluded as a child. I was included in family activities and participated age-appropriately in home skills. I felt alienated only when I first came to the United States, but was able to join the mainstream life with education and job training. I see how I used my mother as a role model in age. Her passion for volunteerism rubbed off on me and helped me to come to terms with getting older.

The most remarkable aspects of my mother's older years (and now I am remembering the time past her eighty-fifth birthday) was that she remained fiercely independent and never asked for help directly. I tried my intuitive best to remember what items of groceries she might need, which doctor's appointment was due, so that I could be available and ready to help her. She tried to do it all alone. My eyes started seeing little things, like whether the garbage can needed emptying, empty bottles needed to be recycled, dry cleaning taken care of. My mother and I developed a more tender and loving bond than ever in our lives. We combined doctor's visits with pleasant and relaxed lunches, picking up medications with short trips to the mall. My mother always stopped at the Hallmark store to get cards for her grandchildren and friends. There was always time for that. No rush. We, my mother and I, communicated spiritually, and it sometimes only took a blink of an eye to know what the other was thinking.

Her first heart attack occurred the morning after her ninetieth birthday party. I noticed the night before that she had trouble blowing out the candles and was short winded. She went home and did not complain. I thought she was only tired. The next day, on the way to the emergency room, while she was propped up in a sitting position on the gurney, she was still alert enough to notice that they were mopping the hallway floor and caution us to be careful and not to slip.

I realized that getting older is an ongoing process. It starts in childhood. One learns how to manage one's life, family, and job. One becomes a pro at it and before one realizes, grey hairs have multiplied, one's back is getting a little stooped, and eyesight is a bit blurred. One should not be afraid to look into the mirror and accept oneself. The world will smile back at the person who does not carry a chip on his or her shoulder and does not have misgivings.

The Passing of an Era

On Wednesday I saw the obituary. Harvey Black, my old boss, had died. It was sudden. He had slipped in the bathroom and fatally injured himself. The account of his life included his formal education and named his five children. He was a pollster of famous politicians, some of whom were elected to office and others who fell by the wayside. He was credited for his abilities with exit polls and sophisticated sampling procedures.

A flood of memories came rushing into my mind. The Harvey that I knew was a loveable rogue, a master of the sleight of hand. He could manipulate numbers to prove his point. If people disliked a candidate in Fresno, he would stress the positive profile in San Francisco. If the full quota for a project was not met, he would weight the completed interviews so that, for example, eighty interviews stood for the answers of a hundred people. If it rained on election day, he adjusted the percentages because he knew that women were less likely to go to the polls in bad weather. So his predictions would not falter or be threatened. The payroll was due on the first of the month but the amount of money he deposited might cover only half of the checks issued—his employees made a beeline to the bank on these days so that their own paychecks would clear. Harvey was always charming, clever, witty, and personable. He wrote funny memos to the staff. He always had the best coffee roasted for the coffee breaks. However, he did not remember names.

My job was to hire and supervise the interviewing staff. He installed telephones in the basement of a residential building, many soundproofed booths with long-distance telephone lines. I was asked to buy my own desk, chair, and the lighting fixtures on the first day and charge it to the company. We had a trained staff of twenty in one month's time. All my previous experience of networking, enticing staff from other marketing companies and want ad advertising came to be utilized. My staff were bright, well educated, and poor. They needed to earn money. They were college students, housewives, hippies, or older people. They liked the flexibility of evening working hours. They were interested in political issues. Their training involved role playing, interviewing each other, doing practice runs of previously used instruments, and familiarizing themselves with geographic components of the State of California, since most of the polls were done statewide. Probing techniques were discussed—how to sound professional and how never to give biased or leading questions to respondents. The work was steady and the interviews increased as the political races heated up. Daily quotas were raised, and the pressure was difficult to keep up with. New staff were hired as some of the steadies dropped out for exams or other personal reasons.

The seasons changed. Time went by. The Xerox machine broke down, outside resources had to be used to get the questionnaires ready. The interviewing operation ended when the candidate that Harvey predicted would win lost the election. His credibility suffered a fatal blow. Also, at the same time, the lease ran out on the office space. Harvey closed a chapter in his life and went on to a new venture.

The memorial service was to be held on Friday at 1 p.m. at the Unitarian Church. I decided to pay my last respects to Harvey.

The courtyard of this old wooden chapel was in full bloom. Irises opened their purple petals. Pansies shimmered in the breeze. The room was full. Well-dressed men and women sat in the pews. There was a wood fire burning in the old fireplace. Candelabras were lit on the sides and front of the chapel. The candles cast an eerie glow on the crowd, other worldliness, and mysteriousness. It reflected his busy and adventurous life.

I was roused out of my reverie by the entrance of the minister. His dark robe was adorned with a white vestment. He clicked on the electric light at the pulpit. The organ was humming soothing melodies in the background. Bach fugues, I think, or Scarlatti harmonies. The minister cleared his throat and began to speak.

"We are gathered here to celebrate the life of a man we knew. He was honest, hard working, a good family man, and a generous supporter of this church. We mourn his loss and carry his memory in our hearts...."

After the minister and other memorials, the organist concluded by singing "Amazing Grace." The crowd dispersed to the social hall to sip wine and sample fruit and cakes.

All of Harvey's children were present. Martha now lives in Cairo and works for the International Agricultural Advisory Board. Mark is a lawyer in Berkeley. Steve married a British classmate and works on Bond Street. Jason was still a graduate student at an Eastern college. They all looked handsomely dressed and well groomed. I heard that the oldest daughter, Amy, lived with a Hispanic gardener and was expecting her third child. She was there, heavy with child and the weight of her pressured, difficult life. She moved slowly and did not smile. And it was Harvey's fourth wife who greeted the guests. She used to be his secretary and we always enjoyed their flirting exchanges. After the mother of his kids died, six years ago, Harvey made an honest woman out of Marlene and married her.

Harvey had straightened things out in his life and hopefully, he died in peace. I signed my name at the registry and took a candle to light in his honor.

The Five Angels in My Life

Rabbi Michael Gold, who is knowledgeable about Jewish mystical tradition, points out that there are certain souls to whom we are connected in a profound way. Perhaps it is the soul of our spouse or lover, the soul of our parents or children, or some other family member. Perhaps it is the soul of a close friend and confidant. Or perhaps it is the soul of a person we meet by chance encounter, who helps us correct the trajectory of our lives.

God sends such people to us to help our soul fulfill its particular mission on earth. Perhaps there are people we meet because, on some spiritual level, we are meant to meet them. We are already connected to them on a spiritual level. (Citation by Rabbi Larry Raphael, from his sermon on "Chance Encounters," February 2009.)

There have been five people who unexpectedly set the course of my life. When I met them I was not aware of their important roles and their lasting effect in decisions I made later on.

When I was sixteen, my parents sent me to apprentice at the photo studio of Tibor Csorgeo. My father, Zoltán Biró, was employed by Forte, the Hungarian subsidiary of Kodak. Forte contracted with several outstanding photographers, whose works were used to promote company products. Mr. Csorgeo was a prize-winning specialist in outdoor sport and action scenes: pretty girls riding bicycles, gymnasts jumping, and such.

One afternoon, after a business meeting, they had a private talk and I was accepted as an apprentice. My mother walked me to the master's studio, close to our home, a modern apartment on Szalay utca in Budapest. Mr. Csorgeo, or, as he like to be called, Uncle Tibor, was friendly and welcoming. He showed me his darkroom and portrait studio. We started by looking through albums of his work. Then he showed me how to develop black-and-white film, enlarge pictures, take portraits with the use of backlight, avoid shadows, and diminish blemishes and soften facial expressions. I loved each day, each new discovery. Eventually I became one of his models. He used the portraits to advertise his studio. I recall that he had a display in the entry hall of the apartment building. I became a passionate observer of capturing shadows outdoors, always looking for interesting angles and unique shots of genuine facial expressions. Nothing was too bizarre or ugly. It was all real, to be captured on film and preserved. Our relationship ended when I left Hungary to come to the United States. The last photos I received from him were those of my parents trying to smile bravely, missing their daughters, whom they were not sure they would ever see again. He captured a bittersweet moment then, there. He remained an angel in my life after all the decades in between. Photography remains one of my passions to this day.

The second unique hero in my life was Juci Schulz. She was the director of refugee services in Wien, Austria, where we fled to from Communist Hungary. She had relatives in Budapest who knew of her appointment at the Joint Distribution Committee to handle the influx of Hungarian émigrés who were crossing the borders to escape the Stalinist oppression. Her relatives, friends of my parents, thought she would help us in Wien that cold, rainy winter when we arrived on foot with just the clothes on our backs.

First, she sent us to the used clothes distribution center, for warm sweaters, gloves, scarves, hats. Then she sent us to the kitchen for a hearty meal. Afterwards, back in her office, she filled out papers, to notify our relatives in the U.S. who would provide us with visas, transportation, and future care, after our immigration to the United States. At present we were stateless, *stadtlose,* undocumented aliens. Gradually, she considered our other needs: school enrollment for my sister, who was thirteen years old then, and an occupation for me, seventeen at the time. She needed help in her *kinderhaus,* a shelter for refugee babies and toddlers. She gave me a job as a nursemaid, and I learned to care for infants and small children.

Mrs. Schulz, or Jucineni, was a widow who lived in Austria after the war. Her two young children, a boy and a girl, had died recently, after a typhus outbreak in one of the refugee camps. She was still bereaved and wore a cloak of sadness wherever she went. Somehow she managed to put her personal losses aside to help the needy. Her reputation was that of honesty and tireless generosity with her time and energy. She came to her office early and left late, after all the loose ends were tidied up. She became my all-time role model, as an effective and broad-minded administrator who regarded her clients' dignity at all times.

We remained friends for decades to come, after we left for the United States, with personal visits to each other, letters, and phone calls, until her unfortunate and untimely death in 1985 from lung cancer. Her memory is etched deeply into my heart. Our lovely granddaughter carries her name with pride (Julia Rothblatt, in Los Angeles).

Then came college in the United States. The heroes of my teenage student days were my teachers, Jeremy English and Frances Etheridge. They opened new horizons for me, not only in the reading and understanding of English literature, but also by being independent, strong, self-sustaining women. I was brought up to think of a household as a husband and wife, and one or two children. Well, at Rockford College, I found that two women together make a family and a team, too.

These two ladies had a lesbian relationship for twenty-five years. Each was a professor of English. They shared a house and housekeeping responsibilities. Miss Etheridge did the domestic chores while Miss English took care of the bookkeeping and management of their incomes.

Miss English was a published poet, and she was currently working on a big volume of her collected work. I was invited to poetry reading evenings at their house. "Nicky" Etheridge served hot punch and cookies, and my student friends and I sat at their feet listening and absorbing the atmosphere. I broadened my understanding of lifestyles and boundless possibilities of self-expression. However, I did not become a poet.

The next hero in my life was not an angel. He came close to being a devil. After a lifetime of honest work and diligent honesty, I encountered selfishness and exploitation, manipulation and deception. Harvey ran a political-polling business and gave me the opportunity to be his fieldwork director. Harvey was a New York–born maverick, who created a random sample of voters, based on voting patterns and zip-code data, which he used for telephone surveys. The task for interviewers was to meet a large, predetermined quota, calling statewide to track the pulse of the public. The data was tabulated nightly, and thus the staff had to burn the midnight oil even after the public was sound asleep.

It was a superhuman effort to do this for several months. My job was to set up a telephone center where twenty-five people would dial state-wide to feel the pulse of the voters. The business was housed in the basement of a residential building, overlooking the North Bay. Harvey's office was above mine. He had the view of the blue water and the cloudless sky. Ours was underground and poorly lit. When he first hired me, he would give the interviewers headlamps to work by, like the miners had. It was very much an upstairs, downstairs class structure. Yet the challenges of making it work excited me and urged me on.

After I purchased secondhand furniture for my own office, we moved on to installing the phone cubicles for the interviewers. Folding chairs were acquired and the phone company put in the twenty-five lines. It took me a month to hire the staff. I had a rolodex full of people I knew and had worked with on previous projects. I had a following: people trusted my loyalty to them and to the job that had to be done, on time and honestly. I had supervised people on other projects and knew how to train people so that they performed without injecting personal bias into the questions asked. When word got out that we were hiring, word-of-mouth networking brought me bright men and women, hungry for paychecks. There are a few people whom I need to mention, people without whom we could not have succeeded: my assistant, Jean, who was tireless and always got the job done, even when she had to burn the midnight oil; Charlie, who charmed the hardest-to-reach "respondent" and brought good cheer to the troops; John, another loyalist, who worked overtime and did not get the recognition he deserved, especially from Harvey.

Why was Harvey a devil? He blamed my staff if the outcome of a poll was not to his anticipation. Later it proved to be the result of other variables, like other measures on the ballot. It was not cheating or improper use of the sample. He fired people willy-nilly. He had a labile financial system. Paychecks bounced, there not being enough dollars in the till to pay everyone, so people raced to the bank to cash their checks while there were still funds in the payroll account. One time, Harvey's car disappeared from the garage. I got an angry call, "One of your interviewers stole my car, Agnes. What are you going to do about it?" I went upstairs and absorbed his barrage of insults. Meanwhile his secretary made some phone calls and came back saying that the car was repossessed for nonpayment of the lease. I tried not to gloat. I kept things going with a smile. My job ended in 1984 when Harvey predicted victory in the Bradley election for governor and the candidate lost. Harvey lost face with his clients. The phone room was closed. Harvey died a few years later after a fall in his bathroom. A very exciting chapter closed in my life, after five years of "being on call." I went to work for a California public health research group in Emeryville and started to probe the environmental effects of pollutants on birth defects and cancer.

My most recent angel is my creative writing instructor at the Fromm Institute. Gabriella is a published author and a Holocaust survivor. She has inspired me to record my life story and share my experience during World War II with my family and friends. She taught me how to write fluidly and without restraint. She made me realize that my story was an important one that should be told. She taught me that including background information and describing details is creating a historic backdrop to a personal story. Gabriella herself is a role model. A woman in her eighties, she lives an independent and gracious life. She looks upon her students as potential talents, yet to be explored, and a treasure trove to be opened. She never lost her enthusiasm about finding latent skills in us not-so-young people. She inculcated in me that there is urgency in writing and remembering the past. Her message rings in my ears and continues my efforts. Writing is my life. Memories should be recorded before they fade into oblivion.

Here is a toast to my angels. Your wings are fluttering gently around me. They make me get off the ground and elevate my spirits.

A Dream of Gerti
Fall 2001

I feel so happy and joyful now. Isn't it wonderful to be home in Budapest again? My friends are all there waiting for me. Gerti looks so youthful, and the lines in her face have smoothed out. Juli is bubbling with good cheer. She is telling me of all her guests that have arrived from Vienna: her violinist friend with his Hungarian wife, and her old school friend who moved to Israel after the war. They all rented a car and are taking a weekend trip to Lake Balaton. They will swim and talk for days.

Juli tells the big news: Gerti has a new boyfriend. He is young, brown-eyed, handsome, muscular, and tall. He works at the boathouse where Gerti keeps her rowboat, at the Roman baths on the Danube, upstream. Gerti also owns a little cottage near there, and the two of them go and have coffee there. A serious romance is in the making. That is why there is a glow on Gerti's face, Juli deduces. They invite me to go on a picnic with them on Saturday. We will meet on the Buda side of the Margaret Bridge and take the local train, HEV, upstream to the Roman Baths. All I have to bring is my bathing suit and a towel. I am reminded that there are Roman ruins nearby, called Acquincum, where you can still see the foundations of old temples and baths. They were unearthed when they excavated a Catholic church, more than two hundred years ago. Ahh, the layers of civilization! A world that has vanished! We are but a speck of dust in the grand scheme of time. I muse. I ponder. I mull history in my mind: the past, the present, and maybe the future.

Then I wake up.

This was all a dream. Gerti is no longer among the living. She died two years ago. Her boat was sold, the boathouse taken over by her students, to whom she left everything.

I sit up, back in my bed in San Francisco, and it is time to get up. I smell the coffee brewing downstairs. My dream put a smile on my face. It is so good to go back in time for a moment.

Life Can Be a Waltz
June 2, 1997

I awoke in a sun-filled room. Outside, warm breezes were moving the white-green branches of the birch trees. Looking through the muslin curtains I could see Edna's flowers as they edged the outside borders of her well-trimmed garden. Irises opened their purple petals, snapdragons reached toward the sun with their yellow and white cups, the ranunculus paraded in purple and pink transparent petals. Birds were chirping cheerfully in the trees as I looked out, and even a daring squirrel darted across the lawn. How perfect, I thought. Time to get up and see what the rest of the household is doing. I quickly brushed my hair, threw on a robe, and slipped on my slippers.

I was ready to give a hand in the kitchen. There were lots of people there already: young women finishing the icing on the wedding cake. Alyson was smoothing cream cheese frosting on the towering layers. Another brown-haired, tall girl was washing flower petals—pansies that will decorate the cake. Somebody else was setting up champagne glasses and an ice cooler.

Edna, our hostess, was pouring coffee into eight ready cups. Sam, our host, was slicing coffee cake. This group effort was to get us ready for the big event ahead, to fortify us as we began the day, the wedding of our children. Our nephew Jim was marrying Lizzie on Long Island, in a garden ceremony that they had planned.

There was good cheer in the air and happiness abounding. We have been planning for this moment to come. We were ready to walk them down the flower-hedged aisle to seal their union. The wedding canopy was in place at the far end of the garden. Ribbons flowed from its corners.

Just then the musicians arrived, promptly as expected: three violin players, one college friend with an urdu, and Melinda with her gordonka. They tuned their instruments and started a quick rondo then switched the melody to a *csárdás*.

I could see there will always be harmony and melody with this union, and if a moment of dissonance sounds, it will be turned into a polka or a waltz.

I saw them in my dreamy vision twirling around the kitchen counters and flying into each other's arms with a lovely flash in their eyes, a couple in love.

Forgive Me

"Will you ever forgive me?" said Eddie to Peggy on the telephone. He was calling her at home, in New Orleans. They had parted only hours ago, at the San Francisco airport. Eddie felt very sorry that he and Peggy were unable to reconcile their problems. He regretted that he let her return home instead of staying in San Francisco and marrying him. He wanted forgiveness.

They had met six years ago at an architectural firm called Smith & Lawson. Peggy was a senior designer and Eddie was a novice architect just out of school. Peggy, a perky blonde, took a liking to the shy, handsome man. They had lunch together, then they attended a seminar, and soon they were dating. Peggy liked to go to jazz concerts; Eddie introduced her to opera and symphonic music. They explored the restaurants in the neighborhood. They both liked seafood, and their weekly treat was jambalaya night at P.J.'s Oyster House. The music was loud, the people were cheerful, and the food was spicy. Just like home for Peggy, a New Orleans transplant.

Eddie and Peggy took long weekends in Mendocino, and they confessed their love for each other. Eddie was still reserved and did not want to venture off the beaten path. He was not a risk taker, whether it was the type of food he ate or the side trips they took. He liked to stay close to the main roads. He never traveled without reservations at a hotel, and his gas tank was on the full mark when he started. Usually he took an extra set of clothing, just in case. If his shoes got muddy there was a shoe rag in his trunk. Peggy, a woman with free spirit and more abandon, just took one dressy top along with her well-worn jeans. After all, she could always borrow a clean shirt from Eddie.

As the years passed, their twosome became known to others in the office. Peggy turned thirty and Eddie was thirty-two. Now Peggy felt her biological clock was ticking towards the childbearing stage of life. She wanted to have a family now. They had a romantic dinner just then at a South of Market bistro. She asked Eddie what his plans were for the future.

Eddie's answer was, "I am entering an architectural contest, and I plan to spend all my spare time preparing for it. I want to win first prize and have them publish my design in the San Francisco Chronicle. I want to become successful."

Peggy felt as if a bucket of cold water had hit her. She did not say a word. How could their goals be so far apart? She was wasting her time in this relationship. It was not moving in a positive direction. Eddie was a self-centered, egotistical man, unable to make a commitment to her now or in the future.

That same evening she called her parents in New Orleans. She was still close to her family. She loved and cherished her two nephews and had a good time with her brothers and their wives.

"Why don't you come home and work for your dad?" her mother said. "His company is in need of an experienced architect. You could design a new house for us and your dad's construction company could build it. Think about it."

Peggy considered this offer and in two weeks gave notice at Smith & Lawson. She took the course of her future into her own able hands. Eddie could pursue his career without her now.

Peggy was not angry, only deeply hurt. Her loving romance fizzled and could not be mended again. As they say, they had "irreconcilable differences."

Recalling Anita on Mother's Day, 2000

The year was 1953, a long time ago. We were just turning twenty, Anita and I. We were college students in Madison, Wisconsin. I met her at her parents' house when Shike invited me to his house for *Pesach*. Anita was a radiant, blonde, exuberant young woman. Her smile was infectious, and she brought good cheer wherever she went. She moved among the guests comfortably, including Paula and Howard and their baby Paulie, her brother Andy (who at thirteen had just had his bar mitzvah), and some other college students invited that evening. I was impressed by how warmly the family welcomed me, a newcomer to the United States and to Madison. I felt right at home with them.

Shike's dad led the *seder* and, in my mind, I traveled back to Budapest, where my dear grandfather used to sit at the head of the table and point at the *seder* plate, saying, *"Maror. Afikomen. Haroszes. Matzah."* Shike's mom made a wonderful soup. The matzah balls were large, firm, and delightfully uneven, very handmade and individualistic. The gefilte fish was made from scratch. I had never tasted such delicious fish before. The chicken was well baked and succulent, the kugel, sweet and filled with raisins and nuts. Nobody skimped on the ingredients in this home. We sang late into the night, and I had to hurry back to my dormitory to make it in time for the undergraduate girls' curfew.

Later that year Anita and I went to summer school together. We took an anthropology class. Our teacher was Phyllis, a young grad student. She gave the exams and graded the papers while the professor lectured on aboriginal Australia. We took our teacher for coffee after class and found out that she was a European refugee too, from Vienna, Austria, and she had come to Madison after growing up in San Francisco. She took a liking to Anita and me, and we later became good friends and stayed in touch for many years.

Anita was dating and enjoying a nice social life, and my relationship with her brother Shike deepened and became more romantic. Anita was always my friend, and we had many long talks after class. We trusted each other completely, shared confidences, and had no secrets from each other.

When I recall those days, I still see her smiling face and twinkling eyes, a happy memory.

Kata

Her body remained under the ruins for several days. Nobody was strong enough to remove the heavy concrete block that fell on her when the building collapsed in the bomb attack. You could still see her grey skirt, heavy stockings, and her foot. The shoe, not far.

Kata was only sixteen years old. She grew up with her family in the house neighboring ours, at Klotild út 6. The neighbors all knew her since she was a child.

Kata was the daughter of a successful lawyer, Mr. Braun, and his wife, Ellie. They had lived in Budapest all their lives. Kata was a good student and a very obedient daughter. This was 1944, and Kata was separated from her parents. Her dad was in a forced labor battalion clearing bomb debris in some East Hungarian border town. Her mother, Ellie, had been arrested by the Germans as a suspicious dissident because when she went out for her ration of milk and bread, she was cold and put on a coat that did not have the yellow star sewn over the left lapel, as ordered by the Nazis. They put her in a van and nobody had heard of her for a week, although her arrest had been witnessed. So Kata had to make do all by herself.

The bombs and the air raids were frequent now. Sirens wailed day and night. Her grandparents lived next door and she provided them with the necessities, as best she could, but they too were frightened and helpless in this new world of persecution and deprivation. Jews could only go out of their homes between 10 a.m. and 3 p.m. By 10 a.m. all the food was gone. Empty shelves awaited them, so they asked Kata to go to the big boulevard and check on the shops there. Maybe they would have some bones or potatoes to make a warm soup. Kata was not afraid. She said a prayer as she went on her journey.

"Dear God, let me return safely. Let me bring back the supplies we need. I promise not to go out again tomorrow."

She almost reached her grandparents' home. The bomb hit right next door. She could not get to the air raid shelter in time and she could not avoid the sudden impact from the pillar above. When they finally freed her it was too late. The groceries were still in the string bag in her right hand. God did not answer her prayer that day.

Mariska

Mariska was eighteen years old at the time I write of. She had been with our family for six months. She was then a young teenage girl, blossoming into adulthood: blonde, rosy cheeked, with a nice plump bosom, always smiling and cheerful.

She had grown up in the village where my grandfather's vineyard was located. Her parents were tenant farmers with six children; shoes were passed down among the siblings and a bed was shared by three sisters. There was one toothbrush passed along as they washed in the small sink into which well water was poured. Mariska's parents had thought it would be to her benefit to come to the big city and learn how our household was managed. So Mariska's mother packed the family suitcase, made from lacquered cardboard, and placed into it two changes of underwear, two skirts, two blouses, a many-times-mended warm jacket, and a wool cap. They walked to the train station and said their goodbyes.

Mariska was very homesick at first. Then she made friends with Anna, next door, and the two girls walked to mass together every Sunday. Mariska's daily routine at our house was to prepare breakfast for the family. She put on the coffee pot and went to the corner bakery to bring back a loaf of fresh bread and a liter of milk. She would set the dining room table and then she would help me and my sister get dressed. I was nearing six and my sister, Panni, was only two. Later she would take us for a walk. My sister still rode in her stroller. I had to hold on to the side of the stroller so that I would not get lost on the street among the pedestrians.

Once we went to the church, St. Stephen's Basilica, just down the street from our apartment. The church was big and dark with many altars in every corner, where people were kneeling and praying to the Virgin Mary. There were candles burning and the smell of incense floated in the air. I was fascinated by the church but felt like a stranger there. We were not Catholic. We were Jewish. Even at age five I had a sense of illicit curiosity about how "they" worshipped. In our synagogue there were no statues to be seen, no smell of incense to be inhaled. But Mariska was kneeling in fervent prayer, crossing herself as she rose, holding her rosary tightly in her palm as she continued her monotonous prayers. My sister, in the meantime, had fallen asleep in her stroller. It was warm and comfortable in the church's womb-like atmosphere. Mariska coughed as we went outside. She pulled her warm coat tight and felt in her pocket for her handkerchief. I noticed blood.

I liked Mariska very much. I always felt happy when it was time for our daily walks. This time I held her hand as we started to go back home. We took the elevator to the first floor, to manage the stroller easier because Panni was still asleep. When we entered the large apartment we were greeted by both grandmothers. Grandma and Grandpa Szlovák lived with us in the back of the apartment with Grandpa Móricz. They were part of our daily lives. But Grandma Lottie, my dad's mom, was only sometimes with us. She lived across the river, in Buda, with our dad's sisters.

I was very excited to see them both together. They ushered me into a dressing room, a kind of cloak room off the main entrance hall, and they took turns peeling off my coat and boots, removing our outer clothing.

Then Grandma Szlovák said sadly, "Mariska must go home immediately. The doctor just called. They found out that she has tuberculosis. She may be infectious."

In the meantime my sister had been whisked into the nursery

by my mother. We both were bathed and sanitized, gargles were administered, and the bedding was changed. Cups and plates were dipped into boiling water. Toys were thrown away.

I was bewildered, upset, and confused. What is all this fuss? Why do I have to part from my good friend and companion Mariska? Where is the Virgin Mary that she just worshipped? Where is our *Adonai*, my Jewish mentor? Are germs from the Supreme Power? Are we all powerless as we live our daily lives? What can I believe in now, when everything that I know changes in a split second? Whom can I trust?

On that day my innocence was shaken, and nothing quite remained the same.

A Day in the Life of a Little Girl

Julia is in third grade. She moves quickly between her classmates as she picks up her assignment for tomorrow's homework. Her brown hair is flying as she hops and skips to her seat. She has to write a story about her family. Well, luckily her family is small: Dad, Mom, and Shabu, the dog. Her attention wanders to the noises outside. Cars are slowing down and stopping, a dog is barking. I guess school will soon be out. Mrs. Ben-David is telling the students to clean up their workspace and put away their textbooks. Julia whispers to Olivia, her best friend.

"I'm coming to your house for a play date today, right?"

Olivia says, "OK. We can do our homework together."

The bell rings and the class files out the door. Olivia's mom is waiting outside and greets both girls. "We'd better get going, I'm double parked."

The girls skip and jump and soon are in the station wagon. After milk and cookies, the kids watch their favorite show, "Barney," telling them about how to cross the street safely. You have to be careful when you are alone. Don't run. Walk and look both ways first, to the left and to the right.

"My Family," Julia writes. "My mom's name is Jayne and she works in an office. She helps to raise money for children in a home. These kids don't have moms and dads. They are lonely, and teachers take care of them. She goes to work early and comes home late. When she is at home she likes to garden. Her flowers are always pretty. She brings some into the house and puts them on the table.

"My dad is big and tall and strong. He has a mustache. He

works out in the morning. He told me a story about how he quit smoking when I was born. He plays with me and takes me places. We go to the park or for a walk with our dog. Sometimes we go to the pet store and get dog food. My dad works for a university. He teaches big kids. He is very smart. I can tell him secrets. He will listen and never make fun of me or my friends. He cooks on the barbecue. He makes chicken and corn and sometimes steaks, good and healthy-for-you kind of food. I love my dad. I love my mom too.

"My dog Shabu is fun to play with. She never bites, only licks me.

"I have a happy family.

The End."

Olivia comes in and the girls go outside to play.

Soon Olivia's mom says, "Time to go home, Julia. Your dad is waiting outside."

Julia says a quick goodbye and she is out the door. She gets into the car and hugs her dad. He holds his hand out the window. Julia notices that he has a lit cigar that he is hiding from her.

Julia's world crumbles.

"Dad, you promised that you would never smoke again. The doctor said it's bad for your health. You will get sick, Dad. Please. I love you."

A Family Affair

I turn the pages on our family calendars...so many events to recall.

1999: Our grandniece Lauren is born.... The family rejoices.

1998: Our nephew Stefan marries his special girlfriend, Anna.... The family gathers and celebrates their bliss.

1997: My best friend from college, Lizzie, marries her beloved Jim, and both sides of their family travel across country and dance till dawn.... This is a day we will always remember.

My mind goes back in time.

It was going to be an old-fashioned, village-type wedding, the kind they had in the old country, back in Europe. After all, Lizzie and Jim had just finished college and they couldn't afford to rent a hotel ballroom for their union. "Simplicity" was the keyword. "Economize where you can."

The preparations began months in advance of the big day, June 29. The location for their vows was selected by Lizzie. There was an empty lot not far from her parents' country house on Long Island. It was on Long Island Sound, a beautiful setting for a wedding. The lot was empty, weeds were knee high, prickly bushes were blocking the entrance to the open space. And it belonged to Mrs. Jones, a neighbor of Lizzie's parents. So after proper formalities, permission was granted for a one-day use of the wild lot. Of course, it would mean that Mrs. Jones and family would also be attending the ceremony.

Jim and Lizzie spent weekends clearing the land, mowing the weeds, spraying the bushes to free the area of the proliferation of spiders, mosquitoes, and flies that were hiding everywhere.

Next came the arrangements for the reception. If only the immediate families came, the numbers would already hit the fifty mark, and Lizzie's parents' home was only a country cottage. All these people had to sit, even if only folding chairs were provided. They had to eat and drink. After all, they came from faraway places, and they would be hungry and parched. So Lizzie decided to erect a tent in the backyard. She hired a friend who did catering in the area. Her brother offered to be the bartender, and her parents agreed to buy the libations for the occasion. Music is always the most important part of a good party. Luckily, Jim had many musician friends. As a matter of fact, Jim himself was a musician, and he planned to perform with his Polish folk band from New York on the big day.

So things were falling into place. Now the invitations had to be printed and sent out and the guest list agreed upon. Both Lizzie and Jim had many friends from college and from before they both attended New York University. Several evenings were spent debating who would be on the A list (must invite) or on the B list (might invite). Where would the out-of-town guests sleep? Jim's family was coming from Illinois, Wisconsin, Nebraska, and California. Lizzie's mom agreed to put up the parents, and the neighbors had room for the aunt and uncle. The cousins would go to the nearby motel. Even though it was next to the 7-Eleven store, which is open all night, they would be safe at the nearby Sleepy Hollow Inn. There were millions of other details, like the wedding cake.

Lizzie's best friend, Allyson, volunteered to create a cream-cheese wonder with floral decorations. Her sister-in-law was put in charge of the flowers and the bridal bouquet. The local newspaper, the *Southampton Bee*, heard of this unique event and they agreed to send a photographer to cover the happenings. This was news in the community. Nobody had thought of an outdoor nuptial in Southampton before. And Lizzie had grown up in Southampton. She was a *cause cèlébre*. Her family members were well-recognized, upstanding citizens.

The big day came. Everything went like clockwork. Lizzie and her attendants rented a 1956 Chevrolet. They were transported in style to the now florally bedecked, cleared, and manicured empty lot. Jim and his parents came in the family car. Most of the other guests walked from the house to the site of the ceremony.

The musicians were all situated at the far end, near the water, so they could observe the processional. As each group entered, they played an appropriate tune. We, the Hungarians, were greeted with a *czárdas* and nostalgic gypsy folk melodies. Lizzie's dad entered to the tune of "O Sole Mio." Others could be keeping time to a Polish polka or a klezmer village song such as *"Bei mir bist du Schön"* or "Sunrise, Sunset." The wind started up gently. The sun was high in the sky. The wedding party's skirts were blowing colorfully in the breeze. The ribbons on the *chuppah* waved wildly under the clear blue sky.

Under the *chuppah* stood the young couple. They were both moved by the seriousness of the moment. The bride, Lizzie, brown hair smoothed into an elegant knot in the back and complexion glowing, was smiling and radiant. Jim, the groom, his hair slightly tussled by the wind with his *kippah* properly placed on his head, looked a bit shy and nervous. But both seemed very sure and comfortable at each other's side. They were a couple who loved and trusted each other. This moment was what they had planned for and anticipated for a long time, and now here it was. No surprises. They had already made the commitment to each other some time ago and now all that remained was for the vows to be said and recorded.

The rabbi gave the blessings. The wedding prayers were said. The vows were exchanged. Jim stomped on the traditional glass wrapped in a handkerchief. The couple embraced and kissed each other happily.

Mazel Tov!

God bless you.

Have a long and happy life. *L'chaim!*

The whole group danced back to the house. Nobody noticed the pebbles under foot. It was a magic day, a day of togetherness and sharing of joy.

The Architect

He was five years old and started kindergarten. He was one of twelve boys in the class of twenty-five kids. He was a quiet boy, and he smiled when the teacher at the West Portal Elementary School brought out the brown butcher paper, pencils, and paintbrushes. Today the class would be drawing themselves. He measured his own arms and legs with the ruler and started to draw the outline of his own body with the measurements. He looked at his torso and with a sure hand drew the lines, first a sketch, then a secure line. He wore a long T-shirt and skinny-looking jeans. He had on brown shoes. He used the watercolors to make the top peach-colored, even made the star design on the front in black. He finished the features of the face. He stood up and looked at the table when his likeness was completed. He smiled and said, "I like the way it turned out." His teacher, Miss Pond, gave him a crown as recognition for the accuracy and the life-like figure he had painted. His drawing was the best in the class. His mother framed it and put it on the wall. "This boy is talented and should be encouraged." She still has it hanging.

A few years later he was in junior high school. Now he was taking "industrial design." His teacher was demanding and tough. He expected the boys and girls to complete a design of a house in one period. He would specify, "This is a two-bedroom, ranch-style house for a family of four in the suburb of a big city. It is 2,500 square feet in size. There is a small yard and a one-car garage. Now go to work." Our boy had a drawing ready before the others had even started. He had it all visualized in

162

his mind and down on paper shortly. The rooms were large enough for two beds, the traffic flow from entrance to living space easily managed, the kitchen had the appliances placed where the cook could access them easily and deliver the meals to the dining area. The bathrooms were well spaced and the plans all "hung together." He got an A on most projects, and Mr. Schultz, his teacher, encouraged him to consider becoming a professional designer.

In high school he entered citywide competitions and his models won yearly prizes. His eye for using space judiciously and creatively made his models simple and attractive. For the exterior he used bold lines, but it was always aesthetically pleasing to the eye. There was harmony and balance between the roofline and the windows. The entry door looked just right.

Soon our man was in college at the school of architecture in Berkeley. Some tough challenges were given to the students, and many overnights were spent on models for future houses. He was given a narrow lot where two apartment houses were to be built side by side. He visited the lot, measured it, took photographs of the surrounding buildings, surveyed the lot, and then went back to his drawing table and started to work. He was now using a computerized program, the CAD system. When he was finished, two slender buildings shared the narrow lot and there was enough space for the residents' comfort. There were parking spaces under the house balconies on the second floor, planters around the entrance, and an arched entrance. It looked nice enough for young and old people to move in.

He finished college with honors.

With resume in hand, he was ready for his first job. He was an architect now.

There was Frank Lloyd Wright, later Frank Gehry, now the top man for the job is Andre Rothblatt, Architect.

Cooking with Raul
To the Heart, Through the Stomach

"I want to learn to cook some Hungarian dishes so that I can surprise everybody when I go home to New York," said Raul.

Raul was visiting us, his parents, in San Francisco. He was thirty years old, recently married, and a musician. He was a tall, slender, and fast-moving young man. His movements were like ballet turns, as he started to gather some of the pots and pans from the cupboards.

"Let's take the family cookbook and make some selections that we could do today," I said.

Raul went to the shelf and paged through *Flavors of Hungary,* written by Charlotte Biró, my mother, his grandmother.

"How about deviled eggs, layered potatoes, vegetarian bean soup, and walnut pancakes?"

I was delighted with his choices. They were all simple, easy-to-follow recipes. The only equipment missing was a good, reliable crepe pan.

"Let's go buy a good pan, said Raul, "and then we'll succeed."

Grandmother used to say that was the secret of her light and fluffy pancakes: that she had the right tools to make them with. The crepe pan should be a lightweight aluminum, just a large enough surface for a three-inch round crepe. So Raul and I went off to the nearest household supply store to get the missing pan.

"Raul, I'll buy one for you to take home so you can make breakfast when you get home."

"O.K., Mom, sounds good to me. How about the walnut

filling? What should we use for this mixture? We'll need chopped nuts, sugar, and raisins."

"Raul, since time is short and our tasks are many, let's just get some ready-mixed Nutella as a spread to fill the crepes with."

So home we went to start the project.

"The secret of cooking is to have all the ingredients prepared for later use," I said. "Let's boil the potatoes, hard-boil the eggs, mix the crepe batter, soak the beans, and chop the vegetables to be sautéed for soup. Then we'll have a head start on everything."

"It's quite a bit of work, you know," said Raul as we began to chop. "I wonder how Grandma could do all of this when she cooked? She never looked tired when the guests came. She always had the table set with flowers in the middle and lace doilies under the dishes. She always wore her party dress and a flowered scarf around her neck. The house always smelled so good when we entered. I recall a vanilla fragrance in the air.

"Here, I chopped two onions, three carrots, and three ribs of celery. How much oil should I use to simmer all this?" asked Raul.

"Try about three tablespoons, and see if it covers the bottom of the pan. Also, add the parsley and the garlic too, so the flavors will all blend," I said.

"The eggs are ready now and soaking in cold water. What do we need to do with them?" Raul asked.

"Put out the mayonnaise, mustard, white ground pepper, and the capers. After you rice the cooked yolks, you will mash them with three tablespoons of mayonnaise and a tad of mustard. Add the capers as a decoration."

"OK, do you like this consistency?" asked Raul.

"Looks just right," I said. "Lets move on to the layered potatoes now. First, butter the sides of the Pyrex dish so the potatoes won't stick to the pan. Then peel and slice the boiled potatoes."

At that moment the phone rang.

Raul answered it. "Hi, Andre. What's up with you?" It was his older brother on the phone. "Are you coming over tonight? We're cooking a Hungarian dinner. We're using Grandma's cookbook. It seems so easy, with her recipes and Mom's instructions. It's amazing how helpful hands-on instruction is in learning to cook.... Oh, you have other plans. I'm leaving for New York later tonight. Bye then. Hope to see you in New York in April. Maybe I'll cook a meal for you when you come."

He hung up.

"Back to the crepes."

We beat the eggs, added the flour, the milk, and a bit of cognac. The mixture looked lumpy and thick.

"Here, look. The cookbook suggests adding milk if the batter looks heavy. Let's do it. Maybe it will help."

Painstakingly, we heated the new crepe pan and tried to make the pancakes. They were thick and rubbery at first. Later, as we decreased the amount of batter, the crepes started coming out more like what we remembered from the old days: a fluffy, pleasant, fragrant round. I began to fill them lightly with the nut spread, while Raul sprinkled vanilla sugar on top.

"Time for dinner. Soon we'll have to leave for the airport," said Raul.

He packed his gear and hugged his mom.

"Hey, the house smells almost like it did at Grandma's. There are vanilla and good vibes in the air."

Fancy Pancakes with Nut Filling and Chocolate Sauce
(Dios Palacsinta Csokolade Martassal)

Pancakes
4 eggs
1½ cups sifted all-purpose flour
2 cups milk
1 teaspoon brandy
1 teaspoon oil
pinch of salt
melted sweet butter for frying

Filling
1 cup milk
1½ cups ground walnuts
4 tablespoons sugar
¼ cup raisins
1 tablespoon grated orange rind
2 tablespoons rum

Sauce
4 squares Baker's semi-sweet chocolate
2 tablespoons sugar
1 tablespoon cocoa
2 egg yolks
1 teaspoon flour
¼ cup milk
1 tablespoon rum

Combine all ingredients for pancake batter and beat well. Cover and let stand for 1 hour.

Heat a 7 x 7-inch crêpe pan until moderately hot; lightly butter. Remove pan from heat and pour in 2 to 2½ tablespoons batter, or just enough to cover bottom of pan. Immediately tilt pan back and forth to spread batter thinly and evenly. Fry pancake over medium heat until lightly golden on bottom. Loosen edges with a spatula, turn pancake, and fry on second side. Repeat with remaining batter, buttering pan lightly each time. If batter thickens on standing, stir in a small amount of additional milk.

To make filling bring milk to a boil in a saucepan, mix in ground walnuts, sugar, raisins, and orange rind. Cook for 2 to 3 minutes on very low heat, stirring constantly. Remove from heat and mix in rum. Spread 1 tablespoon of filling on each pancake and roll up. Put in a buttered baking dish and keep warm in the oven at 100 to 150 degrees.

To make sauce put chocolate, sugar, and cocoa in a double boiler and melt until smooth. Beat egg yolks, flour, and milk together; add to melted chocolate. Heat sauce, stirring until it is thick—don't bring to a boil. Add the rum. Immediately pour sauce over each serving of pancakes. (This sauce cannot be reheated.)

This dessert can also be served flaming by adding warm rum and igniting.

Serves 6.

Coffee at the Gerbeaud, a Fantasy

Father called me at the hotel the morning after I arrived. His voice sounded deeper and more serious than I remembered it. The warm resonance seemed to have disappeared.

He said, "Ágikam, I can hardly wait to embrace you. It's been so long since you left. Could we have coffee at 11 a.m. at the Gerbeaud pastry shop? It's easy to reach with the #2 streetcar. You remember it's in the center of town, at Vorosmarty tér. We will be waiting for you there."

I recalled that chilly November morning when Father took us to the train station. My sister, Panni, and I had our small overnight bags with extra shoes and warm sweaters ready for the illegal border crossing. We took the train to the town of Sopron. Then we were to cross into Austria and to our freedom on foot. We said goodbye then, hoping to meet again a few weeks later in Wien. At that sad moment we did not anticipate the events that would separate us for fourteen long years. The year was 1950. Panni and I made it successfully to Austria over the minefields and past the search lights and barking guard dogs that controlled the military zone.

Our parents tried the same route with the same smugglers. Instead of getting out, my parents were arrested, tortured, and jailed for many long months. The smugglers got drunk the night before my parents crossing and bragged about their business venture to a secret policeman who was at the same inn. When our parents arrived at the secret meeting place, the police were waiting and apprehended them instantly. A mock trial was followed by many cold nights in unheated jail cells. By the time they were released, Father was very ill and needed surgical treatment. He spent many weeks in hospitals and recovered slowly. When they were free to return to their home they found that their apartment had been confiscated by the government. They were considered political aliens who wanted to go abroad. This was a criminal offense under Communist doctrine. Our father and mother eventually succeeded in finding a room to sublet with an old couple. They shared the kitchen and bathroom. They were happy to have a roof over their heads and to be near the medical services that they needed.

And yet, after all they shared, our parents decided to go their separate ways.

The years went by. They thought they might never see us, their daughters who lived in America now. Then the 1956 uprising opened up the Iron Curtain and news could come from the West. People packed their bundles again and fled across the previously sealed borders. Father, who was in his late sixties, was too frail and too old to start life anew. He settled into his sublet room and worked as a night watchman at the plant where he had once worked as an executive. Everybody knew him and greeted him heartily as they came and went.

On my first return to Budapest, in 1963, I wondered how the intervening years affected him. Would he be thin or plump? Would his posture still be straight or had his back become stooped? Would he be pale or would he still be rosy cheeked? I could not create a mental picture of him. What had he meant by "We will meet you"? Did he have a woman in his life? I can only visualize him as I last saw him in 1949 at the station platform, waving as the train pulled out. As a young girl, all I saw was my dear, loving father. He was a handsome and wise man. He was my hero then.

I got to the pastry shop. It was well before 11 a.m. I looked through the lace curtain and I saw a smiling, contented-looking gentleman. He was touching a well-groomed, red-haired lady's arm. They laughed at a joke that the gentleman had just told. He was my father. They were having a good time together. Father wore a well-starched white shirt and a jaunty necktie. The lady had a mischievous look in her eyes. She wore her hair in ringlets, and in the back she had fastened a fluffy bow.

I was smiling as I walked into the shop. Heads turned here and there. Slowly, I went past their table and out the back door. They did not recognize me.

Memories Are My Ghosts

Fragments of the past gnaw at my heart. They bring pain. They turn and twist in my subconscious like a sharp-edged knife. I have never spoken about the following. Now the best I can do is to try to chase it away.

One of my living nightmares is when my mother slammed the window on her finger. The cord that held the double-hung window taut snapped, and the heavy window nearly cut off her finger. Ouch and terror. Ouch! Blood! She was alone at home on a Sunday but had the presence of mind to call the upstairs neighbor. He took her to the emergency room, her hand wrapped in a towel. She continued to bleed and was faint. After a lengthy admission process she was sedated and bandaged. The nurse called her grandson who picked her up in an hour.

My husband and I were attending a wedding in another town that day. We returned late that night. As usual I called my mother and cheerfully described the beautiful bride, the elegant reception, and how we danced several waltzes. She never let on to what she had been through that day.

That episode has haunted me ever since—not her gentle death years later, but this silent suffering that she kept to herself.

The Arrival

Sári packed her comb, hairbrush, and face powder into her well-worn toilet bag. Her cabin was small, with the sink in the corner, and there was just enough room for a narrow berth and a little chair. She was in the lowest deck. The ship was an old Italian passenger liner called the *Vulcania*. This was her tenth day on board since the ship sailed from Cherbourg harbor. Now the rocking boat was going to arrive in New York. The stormy seas seemed calm at the end.

Sári was nervous and excited. At age fifty-five, she would be stepping ashore in her new country, the land of the free, America. Her cousin Leni would be meeting her as she got off the boat, a cousin whom she has seen only in pictures—brown hair, tall, a young woman who resembled her mother in the photos. She was not sure she would recognize her in the crowd.

Leni was rushing home from work in the garment district of New York City. She was in the designing and cutting department, along with fifteen other young women. Today the boss gave them "rush" work—the fall line had to be cut and the samples had to be shipped to the department stores.

She was almost finished when the sewing machine broke down and each dress had to be stitched by hand. What a bother! She would be late to pick up her cousin, who was arriving from Europe. She decided to get help from her friend Rosella.

"Please get these yellow size 12s done for me, before Mr. B. sees me leaving, won't you Rosie?"

Rosie, her friend, put the dresses under her pile and quickly ran the machine over the seams so Leni could leave.

Leni was out of the shop in a flash and on her way to the subway. She had to get home and change her clothes from her wrinkled cotton dress to a more elegant suit. After all, first impressions count, and her cousin should see her like the well-dressed New Yorker that she hoped to be. Some day.

She took her dad's car out of the garage. In Queens, people only drove their cars on Sundays and special occasions. Luckily, her dad made sure that the gas tank was full. She was already on the bridge when she realized that she only had some change in her purse, three quarters and a couple dimes. She blushed at the thought of having to borrow bridge toll from her newly arrived cousin. But there was no time to turn back now.

At the gangplank the steward loudly announced the arrival of the ship *Vulcania*. All passengers were to debark and stand at the alphabetical post marking the letter of their name and wait for their relatives.

Sári saw the large "B" and struggled with her heavy suitcase to the far end of the wharf. Her feet felt rubbery and unsteady as she made her way down the narrow gangway. People were pushing, shoving, yelling, cursing, trying to get past her. All were trying to find their loved ones. Babies crying, Italian, English, German spoken, right and left. It was a bewildering, noisy chaos.

Soon the crowds thinned and she was among the last to wait under the letter "B" signpost. Sári was almost in tears, worried about being left behind in this strange, new world. Just then a smiling, brown-haired young woman came up to her.

"Bist du meine cousine, Sári? Ich bin so froh dass du gut angekommen bist."

The two embraced like sisters who had finally found each other, never to be parted. They laughed and cried and talked in English and German, trying to communicate their many emotions. Sári felt at home in the arms of her strong cousin, who helped lug her suitcase to the car.

Leni again checked her purse, then remembered that she had tucked a "lucky dollar bill" under the mirror for emergencies. They could go home now.

Reweaving Old Fabric

Here I am at last in my magic little room, far away from the noise and clamor of the city. I have left Van Ness Avenue with its wailing ambulances, honking cars, and yelling people. I can be quiet in this serene space, where trees are my companions, birds wake me, and buzzing flies lull me to sleep. My room is painted pale blue.

The cabinet in the corner was painted with hearts and flowers by a friend. It was a wardrobe that my mother had used in her latter years for coats, purses, and shoes. The coats had been tailored in Budapest some fifty years before and had then been packed in her steamer trunk for the overseas voyage to America. She had come prepared for the New World, where she did not expect to find tailors or shoemakers like those back in her home country. There, she had known every craftsman in the Fifth District. They had fitted her and made her a durable wool suit with lining and padding so she would not be cold in the winter. She was going to join her daughter in Wisconsin, where it is even colder in the winter than in Budapest. Her shoes had been made in Budapest, with a mold that Mr. Adorjan kept to fashion footwear for Mme. Biró. His proudest creation was a stack-heeled shoe made of snakeskin, grey to match her grey fox coat. Mme. Biró had been the trendsetter in her crowd. Her husband, bank president Zoltán Biró, had proudly shown off his wife on the Danube Promenade before they sat down for an espresso at the Corso Hotel.

Once in America, Charlotte Biró became a nanny for a wealthy family. In Wisconsin there were few jobs for a woman well into her fifties. Her *curriculum vitae* included the facts that she played piano and spoke four languages. But she did not drive a car nor could she type to do office work. She settled on taking care of a three year old and teaching her how to play "Twinkle, Twinkle, Little Star." And yes, she could read *The Little Prince* to her charge in the original French version.

Decades passed. Our once new immigrant, Charlotte, eventually left the service of others. Her friends and neighbors found that she had brought other skills from her native country. She could bake a fine sacher torte, and her Ischler cookies came with perfect chocolate icing. At first she baked for her friends' parties. Then, as her orders increased, she baked for the corner delicatessen. Then she had to hire help to do the shopping and cleaning. When she turned sixty-five, she rented a storefront and sold her baked goods to the public. At seventy she bought a family home, and her life story was published in the newspaper. She became a role model for refugees who were starting out in the United States of America. At the urging of her family, she wrote her memoirs and old family recipes. She found a publisher who edited it and who provided her with an artistic illustrator. *Flavors of Hungary* became a bestseller in its genre. The income it brought made it possible for Charlotte to travel, to see all the cities she had dreamed of: Paris, Rome, Florence, Venice, and Wien. Finally, she returned home to Budapest, where she was met at the train station by friends clamoring to see her, kiss her, and hug her. Twenty years disappeared in a moment. She was back at home again with people who knew and understood her.

But now, in my magic room, I have been able to let my imagination escape all boundaries, and I have taken a trip with my mother.

Alas, the solitude is interrupted. A neighbor has rudely turned on his electric leaf blower at full speed. I am back to reality with a sudden jolt. Heaven? Paradise? No, Glen Ellen on a spring Sunday. One cannot altogether escape.

My Mother: Sári Szlovák Biró

My mother lives in the center of my heart. She has been my guiding light, the sun that warms and embraces the universe. She is a blinding, powerful source of energy, a person to emulate and revere.

There are two photos on the wall of my bedroom: my mother as a young girl and my mother as a grey-haired matron. They both reflect a smiling, welcoming, kind person.

My mother grew up at the turn of the twentieth century. She was born and raised in Budapest, the youngest of three siblings. She was the only girl. Her two brothers, much older, were strong, mischievous pranksters. Her father, a merchant, was a true patriarch. He ruled the family with strong discipline. Her mother was an intellectual who read Goethe and Schiller in her spare time.

The family lived in a comfortable flat near the main railroad station. Family legend has it that Grandfather often brought home tired travelers from the trains, who spent the night in the apartment's spare bedroom. Grandfather was a traveler, too. He went to distant farms to buy lots of cattle for the local butchers to slaughter.

My mother, called Sári, became my grandmother's right hand, preparing meals, entertaining guests, looking after the men. She was bright, witty, and attractive, and everyone's favorite. In 1914 the First World War broke out. Her two brothers, Béla and Andy, went to the Albanian front as cavalry officers. (I found out that well-off families all provided a horse for their sons as they went to battle, to protect them from being shot at as foot soldiers.) Sári baked cookies and wrapped packages for her brothers at the front, and wept at night as she prayed for their safe return.

At age twenty-one she married my father, Zoltán Biró, an aspiring bank cashier. The two families, the Birós and Szlováks, were family friends. Both families came from the wine-growing region near Lake Balaton, and the marriage was blessed by the two sets of parents. After a glamorous honeymoon in Nice and Paris, Sári and Zoli settled into an elegant apartment in Budapest.

I was born seven years later and was raised with love and attention lavished on me. My mother wore a nurse's gown when bathing or diapering me to make sure everything was sanitary.

In 1939 the clouds of war gathered again.... Hungary became an ally of Germany. Jewish persecutions started. As we were Jewish, my mother rose to the challenge. She prepared an escape route for the family, purchased Christian legal documents, found a hiding place, and carried off the rescue with unfailing bravery and cheerfulness. My father was all this time away in a labor camp. The rest of the family hid for months in a suburb of Budapest, until the Russian troops liberated us in early 1945. Our home in the inner city had been bombed. After the war my mother relocated the family to an undamaged apartment and continued with life as we knew it with the limited resources existing at the time.

Communism followed Nazism. My parents were captured while escaping at the Hungarian border and imprisoned. My mother became the prison chef and soon was doling out food portions to the prison warden.

In 1957 she came to the United States, in her mid-fifties. She started a cooking school, published a cookbook, and was interviewed about her success.

As a grandmother she nurtured and educated her grandsons, granddaughters, and cherished great-granddaughter, who received her first baking lesson at age three. She inculcated old-country virtues and values as she prepared her family's favorite meals, until her heart attack, the morning after her ninetieth birthday.

She was a role model to young and old, and her legacy is carried on by her family.

My mother lives in the center of my heart, and she continues to give me inspiration to keep our traditions going.

A Visit

"I have been thinking of her all day."

Julia shook her head and twisted her brown hair loose. She had been looking through a family album. The photographs showed family gatherings around holiday tables and candid snapshots at picnics in sunny wineries. Her dad, a tall, lean man, came in to see what Julia was doing.

"Look, Dad. Here she is when she gave me a cooking lesson. We're making raised dough muffins together. I got flour all over the kitchen floor and she didn't even scold me for my carelessness."

Her dad smiled and sat down near her. Then Julia kept turning the pages.

"Here she is at her ninetieth birthday party."

She looks so pale here but everybody is smiling and cheering for her. Her cake has two candles, a "9" and a "0." It is all marzipan with green frosting lettering.

The next page had her in a hospital bed with oxygen tubes around her nose. She was still smiling, looking beautiful for the camera, but not quite as reassured as before.

Julia shut the album. Her memories were crowding one another in her mind. So much has happened. Her dad brought her back to the present.

"Homework time, Julia. "

Julia completed her additions and multiplication. She did her spelling exercises and she colored her map drawing of the fifty states. She closed her school binder and set it aside.

"Dad, I want to go and visit her. We haven't been there since school started."

"OK," said the understanding parent.

Julia and her dad went to the corner florist. Julia selected two white rosebuds, one young and lovely calla lily, and a yellow freesia. The florist tied a pale pink ribbon around the slender bouquet. Julia penned a note.

"Dear Great-Grandma Nyunyu: I love you. Julia."

Soon Julia was skipping down the narrow path and darted in between two pine trees to find her bearings. They arrived at Great-Grandma Nyunyu's grave, and she put her flowers down. She whispered a hello, blew a kiss, and slowly went back to her dad's car.

The Legend of Ilonka

Legends are written of saints. In my eyes Ilonka was like Mother Theresa, a saint who walked among us in well-worn clothes, a kerchief on her head, and a shopping bag in her hand.

I had known her since I was a child, more than sixty years ago. She had been employed by my aunt and uncle since she was a young girl. She came to the city from a village in western Hungary. Her family lived near the town of Sopron, close to the Austrian border. Her father, a tenant farmer, grew wheat and raised cattle. They barely eked out a living. Ilonka was one of seven daughters, the youngest. Three had gone off to service jobs in the city. The other three married and stayed in the village, helping their parents with the farming.

Ilonka was fifteen when she said goodbye and brought her cardboard suitcase to the train. She was going to be a parlor maid. She was to dust, mop, and polish the floors, clean the silver, change the beds, and do a host of other duties for the Oblaths, a comfortable merchant family who had recently moved into the new family home in the Rose Hill (Rózsadomb) part of Buda. It was a two-family home. The sisters and brother of her employers resided upstairs. One of Ilonka's sisters was employed in the same capacity. Another sister, the oldest, Elvira, lived in the basement unit with her new husband, the janitor. The janitor took care of the garden, the staircase, and shoveled the snow. It was a family-run and family-centered household.

The younger Oblaths, Klára and Sandor, had one son, Jozsi. The older Oblaths had two sons, Laci and George. The two sisters, Klára and Rose, and Rose's husband, Pali, upstairs, had frequent family dinners together. The two sisters would run up and down the stairs to exchange stories about the mischief their sons had gotten into.

Ilonka continued her daily routine and slept in the basement in a cell-like bedroom with a bed and a small closet for her clothes. She never had more than two changes of work clothes, but for Sunday she wore a good dress and new shoes. Sunday was her day to celebrate the Lord. She went to Mass at 7 a.m., then came home to serve breakfast to her master's family, and then returned for 10 a.m. Mass. She always gave her change to the poor and usually brought dried bread and some end-cuts of meat to the old beggar in front of St. Stephen's Basilica. In the afternoon she napped for two hours, then washed her hair and rinsed out her underwear. At sunset she walked down Margaret Boulevard and went to sit in the park, especially on warm summer evenings. Hers was a simple and orderly life. Monday mornings she was back on the job and her only relaxation was to visit with her sisters, upstairs and downstairs. She saw her parents only once or twice a year. Train fare cost too much.

Many years passed. The war came and the Oblath sons were taken away to be soldiers in the Jewish work brigade. The Oblath parents were shipped to the ghetto. Two military lieutenants and their families now occupied the Rose Hill family home. The younger couple kept Ilonka as their maid. They demanded more rigorous order: shoes polished daily, military shirts starched and pressed. The lieutenant's wife treated Ilonka as a lowly servant. She often yelled her orders and snapped her fingers for Ilonka to hurry up. When bombs fell during the siege of Budapest, all residents took shelter in the basement. Before war's end, the two lieutenants and their wives had fled to Austria, afraid of the Russians, who were advancing from the east. They did not want to be accountable for their persecution of the Jews in Budapest.

The Oblaths survived the war, after deprivations and hunger

in the ghetto. They were thin, undernourished, and weak. Ilonka went out and scrounged for potatoes or onions to make soup for them on a makeshift wood-burning stove. Electricity and gas were not yet connected.

Then came communism. The Oblath sons fled West. The old parents remained in Budapest. Rose, the older sister, became ill and died of cancer. Ilonka now took care of the bereaved widower besides her regular charges. She took on additional cleaning jobs to supplement her income. She worked five days a week elsewhere and she still cleaned and cooked and shopped for the three Oblaths. She never dated. Men did not attract her. She still prayed and went to church to gather strength for her hard life.

By 1975 Ilonka had saved up enough money to buy a lot on the outskirts, in the town of Erd. She turned it into a blooming garden. On days off, she planted, watered, hoed, and weeded, from sunup to sundown. She brought in bags of cherries in the spring and apples in the fall.

In the 1980s the two Oblath men passed on and Klára was the only family survivor. Ilonka took care of her day and night. She still slept in the basement but after cooking supper for Klára, she would stay upstairs to keep her company. While Klára sat in the comfortable armchair, Ilonka crouched on a stool in the corner, never forgetting that she was the maid. They talked about family, politics, and about what to cook tomorrow. Ilonka would hide chocolate bars in the cabinet for Klára to find and enjoy, and she always brought back more change from her shopping than expected. She was with Klára when the old lady suffered a fatal heart attack at age eighty-six. When the nephews came for the funeral, Ilonka greeted them with homemade chicken soup. Klára had left Ilonka the apartment in her will, but it took Ilonka three months to feel comfortable enough to move upstairs and sleep in her mistress's bed.

Ilonka always welcomed me, the niece who had gone to

America, with open arms. I always came "home" again, and the Rose Hill house remained my home, as it was when I was young, for as long as Ilonka was alive. Each year, we visited the graves together. She chatted and laughed and we did not notice our own creaking, aging bones. Ilonka died in her sleep last year. She was ninety-five years young.

Her legacy and generous spirit live on.

Facing Disaster

Maggie turned the radio dial to the news station and heard the mayor's terse announcement:

"All residents of New Orleans must evacuate their homes because of the impending damage from the hurricane just fifty miles off the Gulf Coast. This is not a test. It is the real thing. Please leave your homes and gather at the Astrodome, where an emergency shelter has been established. This is a city-wide emergency."

Outside, the wind was whipping the trees and the rain came down in buckets.

Maggie was a thirty-five-year-old single mother. She was a successful architect in solo practice, blonde, petite, with a well-exercised, lean body. She was self-reliant and clear headed. Just now she felt scared and deeply worried. She was trembling inside. Outside was a storm of unknown fury. She would be fighting the elements with her own strength. Should she leave the warm comfort of her well-built wooden house? It has been her haven all these years. Should she expose her child to the unknown: flooding, broken windows, flying debris, the elements whipping at her and her young son? She hesitated, but only for a moment.

Then she took the duffle bag off the shelf and quickly packed into it diapers, baby bottles, underwear, shirts, socks, bottles of water, some biscuits and candy bars, the first-aid kit, a flashlight, and her son's favorite cuddly toys. Henry was still napping in his room with his pacifier in his mouth. He had turned two years and was unaware of the dangers outside facing them both.

Maggie called her mother on her cell phone with a sense of urgency in her voice.

"Mom, we are coming to pick you up. Be ready in fifteen minutes. We need to get out of town right away."

Quickly she got the baby dressed in his water-repellent parka, put her own boots and poncho on, and started to lock up the house. The shutters drawn and light switched off, she bolted the door and got into her SUV with Henry in his car seat. Getting out of the garage was difficult. Visibility was poor and branches and papers were flying in the air. She said a prayer and drove the six blocks downhill to her mother's house. The wind was getting stronger and the road was getting flooded from the heavy rain.

As she expected, her mother was ready—always reliable and reassuring. She put her bag into the van with a cheerful hello.

"We should get out of town on the old country highway towards North 99."

Maggie followed her instruction. As they reached N99 they saw that they were part of a slow caravan. Their neighbors were using the same escape route. The idea was to get out of the city, away from the Gulf, to higher, drier land, out of the eye of the storm. They were bumper to bumper now. Slowly moving ahead, Maggie was pleased with herself, that she had filled her gas tank. The afternoon turned into dark night. The wind did not let up. The rain got louder and stronger on her windshield. Her mom was telling Henry the story of the three bears. They passed through the outlying parishes. All the motels had "no vacancy" lights lit. They drove until midnight and were in Alabama. They remembered a little roadside inn where they had stopped once before, for supper, the Big Bear Diner. They went off the road a few blocks and found it.

Maggie put on her flashiest smile and in her New Orleans drawl said to the man at the desk, "The baby and I need a place for the night, and Mother is with us, too. Can you put us up, maybe?"

The key was handed to her and, as she took it, she slipped him a bill. They had shelter for the night and the café was still open. The cook was on duty.

They were too tired to think ahead, of what tomorrow would bring. For now, they were dry, safe, and fed. That is all that mattered.

Suddenly Ill

Your life changes when illness strikes and it all takes you by surprise. Shike went globetrotting from May to June. First he danced at his son's wedding in Brooklyn, and then flew off to Paris for sightseeing and revisiting familiar places. He visited Montmartre with artists at their easels. He stood in line at the Louvre, dined at the Café Ruc, and strolled down Rue de Rivoli. When he missed the flight to Rome and arrived late, he still managed to join the tour he had signed up for, to see Assisi and other hill towns in Umbria. He took the escalators to the upper town in Perugia, walked the cobblestones in Gubbio. He saw basilicas, cathedrals, convents, pristine herb gardens, and dined on pasta with breathtaking views unfolding before his eyes. He attended lectures on agriculture, spirituality, history, and contemporary politics. He took photos and collected postcards of all the sites he visited.

The time arrived for his departure. He was going back home after the six-week sojourn. The plane was crowded, and he ended up in a cramped window seat. He only got up once during the eleven-hour flight back to California. His neighbors were asleep much of the time, and he didn't want to disturb them. When he got home he fell into bed without even brushing his teeth. He was exhausted and weary. His legs felt leaden, heavy, and swollen. He just wanted to sleep.

Around 3 a.m. a sharp pain woke him. It was in his stomach on the right side. He drank a glass of water and went to the bathroom. He could not urinate or go back to sleep. The pain was persistent and unrelenting. He tossed and turned. No use. He called the medical advice service of his health plan. After about a ten-minute wait, a nurse came on the line. She suggested that he should go to the emergency room right away.

"Don't wait till morning and don't drive yourself," said the nurse. "This is an emergency."

By 4 a.m., with his son's help, he was waiting in the urgent-care reception area. Questions, tests, poking, followed by a trip to the MRI department. By then it was 10 a.m. He was admitted to the hospital and scheduled for a surgical procedure. He had a kidney stone blocking his urinary tract. They were going to do a procedure called a nepherostomy: a tube and pump inserted into the kidney, which would siphon out the urine without it passing through the urethra. It would empty into a plastic bag strapped to his thigh. From a healthy man he became an inpatient. Anesthetized, shaven, with IVs in his vein, an oxygen tube in his nose, monitors attached to his chest, he could not move, speak, or think on his own. All his bodily functions were mechanized. He had no choice. He had to yield to the medical team's wishes.

In a couple of days they got him up and out of bed. He felt weak, shaky, and unsteady on his feet. A wheelchair carried him to the car. His son drove him once more.

Weeks of a new routine followed: emptying the plastic urine bag and worrying about its capacity and occasional over-flow problem, which necessitated changing all the sheets and mopping up in the bathroom. He was self-conscious in public—the tube in his kidney was visible through the shirt that he wore. A nurse came every other day to change his dressing, which was very helpful, for Shike could not reach in the back where all his medical equipment was inserted. He and his male nurse slowly bonded. The nurse now accepted coffee and sat down to chat with Shike about politics and current news events. He asked Shike if he would not mind being photographed for a promotional pamphlet that the visiting nurse association was printing and publishing for new patients.

Well, Shike felt he had come full circle, from world traveler to hospital-bound patient to role model for his peers. "Nothing to sneeze at," he thought. Now if they could only take that blessed tube out of his kidney and he could go back to urinating like he used to—standing up and having no more pain—that was all he wished for.

Henry

We have a friend named Hank. His proper name is Henry but nobody refers to him that way. He was named after his grandfather, Enrique, who came to the Central Valley in 1930 to improve the lot of his family. Hank is six foot two, a straight arrow, a proud man. His hair is white now. His moustache and beard frame his face neatly. There are strong laugh lines around his eyes.

Hank is a fun-loving free spirit. He breaks out in song at every possible occasion. He brings a guitar along to most gatherings, just in case he can use it. He sings Spanish love stories, Mexican lullabies, and Cuban rabble-rousing chants. His favorite pastime is organizing his barbershop quartet and performing at birthday parties, St. Pat's Day celebrations, and Fourth of July picnics. His three cohorts are in their eighties and unsteady on their feet, and their bow ties need straightening. Hank checks them out and makes sure they are ready for the stage. Their songs are upbeat and rhythmic. Hank loves to travel to Mexico or Spain, where his native tongue rolls off everyone's lips. That is true music to his ears.

Born and raised in California, the fifth son of a migrant worker's family, he learned English only when he went to first grade; *la lingua de mi madre* is in his heart. There was nothing to sing about then. Hank and his family of seven—Grandma lived with them too—lived in a wooden shack along with other farm workers. He and his brother José shared a bed, the clothes on their backs, and the plate of food they ate at dinner. It was beans and rice, with salsa and tortillas. But Grandma always put a larger helping on their plate, saying, "You are growing boys, and you need it." They rose at five, were out in the fields by six, and didn't stop until noon. His back was sore from bending, his hands were raw from the hoe he used in weeding the neat rows of beans, tomatoes, and sugar beets that they planted and harvested. At night he would pull out his harmonica and play a tune he had heard on the radio. "Guantanamera" and "La Paloma Blanca" were his favorites. His brother José would sing the alto while Hank played his harmonica.

When he got to high school he worked summers only. He had to board with his Aunt Maria and Uncle Pablo, and he took care of their chickens in return. They lived in Watsonville, where the high school was. He saw his parents and brothers on holidays only.

He liked the Day of the Dead holiday, when they all decorated the graves, lit candles, and the whole family sang along with the mariachi band as they stopped at the gravestones.

Hank won a scholarship to Berkeley to study biology and botany. He wanted to know what makes frogs jump and how bees can pollinate a whole orchard, why bugs can get into the heart of the cabbage plant, and other yet unsolved mysteries of the plant and animal kingdom.

He fell in love with a fellow student, Rosa, and wedding bells were ringing before the diplomas were handed out. After he got his diploma a good job came along at Chevron Chemicals, an eco-friendly pesticide manufacturer. Their aim was to produce non-volatile pest sprays for farm products. Hank was soon getting a prize for his invention. "Bugs Be Off" was a big success. It was marketed around the world.

That was some fifty years ago now. He and Rosa have a clan of their own, three boys and a girl, all grown now, with families of their own.

His happiest times were still when his brother José came to town and he pulled out his old harmonica and they sang the old childhood melodies together. Hank was still the sixteen-year-old adolescent at heart. The twinkle in his eyes never left him, and he always kept Rosa by his side.

A simple life, well lived.

Hat

I wore my new hat to church today. It is a straw hat, all lavender, and there is a big bow in the back part. My granddaughter Amy pinned a bunch of purple violets on it, a bouquet made out of pure silk. It does look pretty. I wore it so proudly that even Pastor Jones commented on it.

"Mrs. Armstrong, don't you look all dressed up today. You even have a naughty glimmer in your eyes. What can you be thinking of? I noticed you during the prayer meeting. You were smiling."

That's a compliment for an old lady my age. I have passed ninety already and I am getting on. If it were not for my gout and arthritis, I would be getting out more often, but all the pain in my joints slows me down. Going down the stairs is especially hard for me. Going to church has become an effort now. But then church means hope and encouragement for me.

To see the young families in the pews, the families with little children, takes me back to Baltimore when I was raising my two, Jane and Johnny. Dressing them nicely made them feel good about themselves. We didn't have much money back then and it was either fixing up my hand-me-downs or making little dresses on my own. My old Singer sewing machine helped a lot. Luckily, my mama taught me how to sew when I was a girl. So you see, my mind wandered back to the olden times. Life was simpler back then, but also pretty much the same as it is now. You hope and wish. You want that your children should be proud and strong people when they grow up, and you give them all the guidance and the strong home ties while you are raising them up. You tell them about the Granddaddy and Grandma who came out of slavery back then, and worked hard for all the freedoms we have now. They would be proud if they could see them all grown up and working at good jobs.

Bless the Lord.

Bless Mama and Daddy.

Zoli, 1963

He put on his new shirt. It was starched and pressed, just as when brought from the cleaners. Today he was meeting Mrs. Kiss, his new boss. She had been appointed by the party boss running the Credit Bank to supervise local branches in Budapest, to make sure that they conformed to political requirements.

The year was 1963. The socialist government held tight control over satellite Eastern bloc countries such as Hungary. Zoli was not worried about his knowledge of the operational procedure, only about his party affiliation. Or shall we say his lack of party affiliation. He had avoided joining the Communist Party though most of his colleagues had entered the ranks of card-carrying loyalists. He was not a Communist and could not pretend to be one.

Zoli polished his well-worn brown shoes once more and nodded his head, "I'll just wait and see." He packed his lunch into his briefcase, sorted through the papers that he was going to present to his new boss, his past awards: "leading employee," "production control," "diligent." He closed his door, locked all five security locks, and descended the staircase slowly. He had been short of breath lately. He attributed that to restless and sleepless nights and to anxiety about his job. "I should see my district doctor as soon as I can take a day off, even though it is a three-hour wait at the clinic to be seen. Maybe next week." He continued to walk slowly, his back slightly stooped. People were waiting at the streetcar stop, so he knew the #6 train would come soon. It did. He had to stand all the way to his office at the end of the line, about twenty-five minutes on the slow ride across the main boulevards of the Pest side of the city.

He was huffing and puffing when he walked to his cubicle on to the second floor of the bank. "Oh good. I am still early." Only two of his younger colleagues were at their desks. He was busying himself with the incoming mail when he heard Mrs. Kiss call harshly from across the hall.

"Comrade Biró. Come into my office at once. I have to review your employment status."

Zoli felt an iron fist grab his heart, a giant vise grip his chest. He perspired heavily. He staggered, overcome by a force that was stronger than what his frightened mind could muster. He lost the ground under his feet. He collapsed, could not move.

"I am going to my grave without joining the hated Communist Party," was his last thought as he closed his eyes. His heart stopped beating. His fight for his job was over.

Zoli Biró was my dad. He died of a heart attack at his office on December 13, 1963. He was buried according to our religious principles, without party honors.

Getting Acquainted
(Overheard July 5, 2009)

She had long blonde hair. Her suntanned shoulders looked pretty and round, peeking out from her yellow-and-black form-fitting blouse. He had a shock of white hair, ruddy complexion, and wore a white polo shirt. He was tall. They sat down at a picnic table and unwrapped their deli-bought lunch on Sonoma Plaza. A loaf of sourdough, some sliced Italian salami, and Sonoma jack cheese. He opened a container of pasta salad. She had some cut-up melon. The both sipped bottled low-cal Nestea.

"How important is religion to you?" she asked.

"Not very," he answered. "My, this salami is tasty."

"Do you go to church often?" she asked.

"Only for weddings and funerals," he answered.

"Well, that's good," she countered.

The two of us, my husband and I, were sitting at the other end of the picnic table, eating the same fare as our new seatmates. We added olives, radishes, and peaches to our baguettes, with salami and cheese.

A boy came by selling cookies, to help sponsor a camping trip. She bought a package and we did as well. Afterwards I approached them.

"Where are you from?" The classic opener.

"Orinda, near San Francisco," she said.

"Oh, we are from San Francisco too," I replied.

They were about ready to walk to their nearby car. She stepped back and asked, "Do you know of a good place to get married around here? We are planning to tie the knot and are looking for a nice cozy place."

"Try the Ramekin," I answered. "It is so romantic. It's to the left, and they are open Sundays."

Bananas

She wore a string of bananas around her waist. When she danced, the bananas bounced and flounced, and she dazzled her audiences at the Cotton Club in New York. The year was 1929 and the upper-class white audience was keeping the beat with the dancing on the stage, while sipping champagne from long-stemmed glasses.

Josephine Baker was the star of the show. She took you by surprise. She was at the end of the chorus line and she would often get out of step, just occasionally. When the others kicked high, Josephine kicked sideways and winked at the couple closest to the stage. She pretended to make a little mistake. After the thunderous applause she would come back and do a solo with more sideways kicks, and she would bring the house down. Josephine was small, sinewy, and her torso could bend as if she were made of rubber. That amazing body was crowned with a pretty face, expressive black button eyes, and a small, roundish mouth. With her sharp mind she was planning her next job. When her contract at the Cotton Club ended she would be in Paris, France. She had a friend there, Monsieur Magot, and he had a café on the Rive Gauche in the Latin Quarter. She planned to work for him, wait on tables by day, and sing and dance at night. M. Magot even had a flat above the bar where she could sleep. She was brushing up on her French when she was between performances.

"Comment ça va, Madame. Bonjour, Monsieur."

Josephine was a happy and optimistic person, until she fell in love with M. Magot. M. Magot was a fortyish, debonair

Frenchman. He could be charming. At first he kissed Josephine's hand and called her *ma cherie*. He poured her champagne in a tall glass when they made the agreement that she would work six days a week and be free on Mondays only. He showed her the little room above the bar where she would sleep. With a devilish grin he said, "I have the extra key, you know, and I will visit you when others have left for the night. Don't worry; I am a very good lover. You will never feel lonely. I will keep you warm."

Josephine thought the little room was stiflingly hot, and when she opened the window, the street noise was loud and relentless. Paris was not like she pictured. She felt like a bird in a gilded cage. She was here but her wings were clipped, and she could not try to fly home because she had no money. She had spent all her savings for the one-way ticket from New York to Paris. She was in Paris now and she might as well make the best of it.

She put her clothes in the drawer and her cosmetics in the tiny bathroom. There was a dripping shower, a bidet, and an old-fashioned sink. No hot water came out of the faucet. As time went on M. Magot grew mean and beat her as if she were a child. He hid her makeup when she wanted to get ready for the show. She had to beg him on her knees, kiss his hands, and cry like a remorseful little girl. She could not act silly on stage. She just followed the routine. She was told not to do any more. Nobody clapped and asked for an encore now. Josephine's bananas dropped off her belt like overripe fruit. She lost her bounce. M. Magot took her *joie de vivre* from her. She became just a plain, skinny dancer who did not smile now, who wore too much eye make-up, and didn't kick high enough to be noticed.

What I Did Last Summer, 2000

I just had an intimate encounter…with twenty-six strangers. We traveled together to places none of us had seen before. We took long bus rides together on narrow roads, went through old towns with flower boxes in the windows. We stopped at roadside cafés and family-run bistros. We clinked wine glasses. We spooned ice cream. We slept in small hotels near railroad stations, and we all admired old church steeples.

Who were these people? They were Betty and Malcolm, Marion and Paul, Mollie Johnson, Charlsie Harris, Helen McKegan, and others; from Colorado, New York, Tasmania, North Carolina, Falls Church in Virginia, and elsewhere— places we might picture in our mind's eye, remote small towns that we can only try to imagine. They were teachers, doctors, probation officers, bird watchers, and more.

We found out about their hobbies and food preferences. We watched their wardrobe change from tee shirts and shorts to formal gowns and shirts and ties. We learned of their debilities as walking canes appeared on strenuous days. We offered cough drops as hacking increased on long journeys. We shared stories about children, grandchildren, previous trips, and past adventures.

I was amazed at how rapidly the group became a friendship circle. We looked out for each other. We waited when some slowed down. We cared, we shared, we laughed.

We wondered at marvels never before seen: the Bayeux tapestry, Omaha Beach, the *"galerie de hauteur,"* the third floor of the D'Orsay Museum, the elegance of dinner at the Louvre, the perfection of the gardens of Villandry, the uniqueness of Mont Saint Michelle, the monoliths of Breton, the chateaux of the Loire, the windows of Chartres, the innumerable wonders of Paris—there could not have been more variety and beauties of French heritage (and yet there are).

We paused.

We packed our bags.

We parted.

Now it is like a perfume lingering in the air, still poignant and haunting, but already drifting away, into oblivion.

Dan's Letter to Julia

Dear Julia,

Tomorrow you will turn eight, the birthday you have been waiting for. Your classmates and friends will come with presents wrapped in colorful papers and fancy ribbons. A big cake will be baked at your favorite bakery, and you will blow out the eight candles. Happy Birthday, Julia! What will be your wish? What is my birthday wish for you?

You are already a beautiful girl. Your hair is wavy and has some gold highlights in it. Your brown eyes sparkle with recognition of all the good things in life. You are growing up rapidly.

Your room is filled with toys, more beanie babies than in the store; your closet holds dresses, skirts, jackets, and shoes that even a debutante would envy. You have a dog, a parakeet, two goldfish, and two active hamsters in a cage. Your bicycle, skateboard, pogo stick, hula hoop, and jungle gym are lined up in the backyard.

You are a girl who has everything that money can buy. Your wishes and desires are on my shopping list, always. I want you to be happy and satisfied.

So what do I hope for you now?

That you will become a person who will think of others, and you will learn to share your toys without jealousy and with all your friends. I hope that you will never become greedy and envious of what others have. You will continue to be satisfied with the clothes that your cousin Jessie has outgrown and her mom is sending to you. That you will give some of your toys to the needy children at the holiday toy drive. Maybe you can offer even that cute teddy bear that you got last year. Being generous of heart gives the giver more than the receiver gets. I hope you will realize this soon, the beauty of *mitzvah*, a good deed that is given from the heart.

And for the future? I wish that you should realize your dreams. You want to be an astronaut, Julia. That is an admirable goal. I will do what I can to help you achieve it. I will help you with your homework so that you will get A's in arithmetic. Did you know that astronauts have to do complicated calculations while in space? They have to make sure that their speed and direction of navigation is right on course. Astronauts have to know about the human body. They have to measure their vital signs and oxygen intake. They have to report accurately to ground control. They have to be attentive and can never daydream. Their eyes have to focus on the navigational charts and keep track of everything.

I think you may become a very fine space explorer. You want to know what is up there in the sky, past the atmosphere, in the stratosphere. You are brave and you like adventure.

We are entering the year 2000. This next century will depend on strong and smart people like you, Julia. This will be your century. You and your peers will refine the computer age. You will bank, shop, email, and communicate online. You will no longer have to leave home to do your work. You are entering a new era of endless possibilities.

All this is in the future. All this said and done, right now, go clean your room.

With all my love today and always,
Your dad

My Hero

He is my hero.

He is strong and steady. Soon he will be forty-three, not a child anymore. His birthday is coming up. He still believes that he can change the world for the better.

He lives in Brooklyn. He adopted his community as his own. He only moved there ten years ago, when he finished college at NYU. Now he is the executive of the Brooklyn Triboro Preservation Action Group. He wants to retain the historic landmarks, protect them from the bulldozers of the developers, a big undertaking. But he is unstoppable.

His recent victory was to declare a Duffield Street residence as a site of the Underground Railroad, a stopover for runaway slaves making their way north: a stately tenement home, three stories tall, with wooden shingles and heavy metal railings leading up to the solid wooden door and with tall windows with peeling shutters to keep unwanted eyes from looking in. It is an edifice worth protecting. Soon a plaque will be placed to commemorate its significance.

My hero is now meeting his team in the far end of the large city, a northern borough. There is more work to be done. More people are needed to join the force. Pamphlets will be posted at all the subway entries. An article will appear in the local newspaper.

My hero is tireless. He is energetic and intelligent. He is not stopping until this challenge is met. The developers must be kept out of the inner city.

My hero is Raul. He is my son.

O Patria Mia

"O patria mia—non piu." "Oh, my beloved country—you are not mine any longer," sang Éva at the rehearsal of Aida. She will be singing the title role in a lyric opera production in San Francisco. She is a well-trained soprano, a well-regarded Verdi interpreter who started singing in Budapest. Her first teacher was Lili Benesh. She later studied the George Ungar method at the Chicago Conservatory.

But Éva was not thinking of the opera as she sang. "Oh my beloved country. Oh my sweet Hungary," she was sighing, *"Magyar orszag."* "Why did I have to leave you?" Her heart ached as she put her own homesickness into the phrases of Aida's lament. Her passion of longing came across in her painfully tender voice.

Her memory took her to that rainy day in November, many years ago, when she and her sister walked to the edge of the village in Sopron and found the way through the woods to the border. There were watchtowers everywhere. The terrain was lit up as if it was daylight. Dogs were barking. Soon they reached the barbed wire fence that separated the territory from Austrian soil. Their guides found a dark spot where they would not be observed from the watchtowers and cut the wire. Éva, with her sister and the others, crawled through slowly and carefully. Her coat got caught and was torn. She pulled it free and gathered it close to her body. They walked many hours through the countryside to the small Austrian village of Mariahilfe. There was a car waiting for them there.

Éva, still a young girl never away from home before, kept

wondering why she had to flee like a criminal escaping the scene of a crime. The answer simply evaded her. She never harmed a soul. The political climate forced them to leave oppression behind and since legal travel documents were not issued to students or young employable people, her parents hired smugglers to take them across to safety and freedom in the West. They spent months in transit camps before being able to enter the United States, but school and a new world opened up for them after their arrival in the United States.

Éva has never gone back to her native country. The Communist regime and later immigration laws prevented her from returning. But in her daydreams she has found herself often back at home. In her mind's eye she sees clearly the view from Pest across the Danube to Buda, when the chain Bridge is lit up at night; the spires of the gothic Parliament building, with the chestnut trees in bloom, along the river; the sound of cooing that the doves sing into her ears on Rose hill; the ding-ding of the #6 yellow streetcar along the boulevard; the pungent smell of the fresh rolls at the corner bakery; the fragrance of garlic and green peppers that emanate from the *gulyas* simmering on the stove; her mother calling her, *"Éva, gyere ide."* "Éva, come here and set the table," when the whole family gathered round the dinner table. She is home again, for a moment.

Shoes I Have Known

Shoes, shoes. Klip-klop. I walked across the bathroom tile in my mother's high-heeled shoes. They were black patent leather with straps in back. My feet were small and her shoes seemed big. I looked at myself in the mirror and smiled. My mother was getting dressed in the adjoining dressing room. She was fastening her brassiere and slipping on a blouse. She eased on silk stockings, reached for the garter, and made sure that the seams were straight. She called out to me.

"Ágika, bring me my shoes. I am ready to put them on. I'll walk down to the bakery. We need a fresh loaf of rye bread. Grandfather is coming home and will be hungry after his long tram ride."

Grandfather managed his vineyard and traveled by train from the village to the city. He was a robust, strong man with a handlebar moustache, wore black boots, and carried baskets full of produce for us to use in the household. Grandfather was our hero. He was smart and he was kind. He always had a little treat for us wrapped in his handkerchief for lack of paper—candy or some nuts, hazelnuts or almonds.

We lived in an apartment house in Budapest near the Danube. The bakery and the dairy store were just around the corner.

My mother was stylish. She wore patent leather shoes even when doing household errands. She wore lipstick and carried a large purse. In my eyes she was the most beautiful woman. She stood tall and walked with her head held high. The years passed, war broke out, and air raids became frequent. When

211

they came we huddled together in a damp, chilly coal cellar. There was no heat.

My mother's feet got frostbitten. She could not fit into her regular shoes. My mother exchanged her stylish pumps for my father's masculine loafers. She wore warm socks and stuffed cotton in the toes of my dad's wider, black lace-up shoes.

Let me mention why my dad was not around to wear his own shoes. He was away with the other able-bodied men of his generation in a forced labor brigade. He was clearing away rubble from the bombings in an industrial park. We didn't see him for a long time. He finally managed to escape from the labor brigade after the siege of the city, when the allied bombings became so frequent that the military hold on the labor brigade fell apart. He walked home from where he was captive.

Grandfather became an old man suddenly. His feet were swollen. He could not put his shoes on. He was ill and tired, worn out from running to the cellar day and night as the air-raid signals wailed away. He was cold, uncomfortable, and hungry.

"I am getting too old for this," he said.

One day he just stayed in bed and didn't get up. He went back to sleep and dreamed about his boyhood. He was walking through the fields and he was barefoot. The grass was wet from the morning dew and the sun was warming his face. The memory of the old days brought a smile to his face. We found him in a state of glory when we returned from the cellar.

The Story of the Two Pannis

The two Pannis lived in Budapest. Little Panni had a big sister. Big Panni had a big brother. Little Panni was thin and frail. She had light-brown hair cut in a short bob. She had a mischievous smile. Big Panni had heavy brown braids and she was tall and pretty like a Dresden doll. She was self-assured and acted older than her years. She understood what was going on in the world around her. Little Panni went to kindergarten. Big Panni was in third grade already.

Both of their families lived in Klotild utca. Little Panni lived on the fourth floor of Klotild út 3/b. Her father worked in the bank at the end of the street. He walked home for lunch everyday and he also walked her to school every morning. Little Panni's mother loved to cook. She made *gulás* and baked strudel, and made *matzah* ball soup. Her big sister taught her how to play games like the Mill and tic-tac-toe. She also had a German governess, who taught her how to recite German sentences and sing songs.

Big Panni's father was an attorney. His office was right there in the apartment. He received clients there and dictated letters to his secretary. Her parents took long walks on the promenade near the Danube. Big Panni's brother was smart, and taught her how to play Monopoly and gin rummy. She had a German governess also, who taught her grammar, and she learned to recite poems by Goethe and Schiller.

Then the war came and both families had to run to the air-raid shelter day and night. They could not go for long walks or play in the park with their friends. No more games of marbles or hopscotch. They had their emergency bundles at their bedside, with a flashlight, warm clothes, a thermos of tea, and a book to read. They read their books with the flashlights in the coal cellar. The next day they told each other the stories they read. Little Panni liked Erich Kaestner's *Emil and the Dectectives.* Big Panni read Dumas's *Count of Monte Cristo.* They both dreamed of peace and the end of bombings and food shortages.

People lined up at the stores because there was not enough bread or milk or meat. The farmers were too scared to bring their products to the city in case an air raid would force them to spend the night in the air-raid shelter and they could not take the train back to their homes. The trains were not running anymore and the city was under siege. The Allies were trying to defeat the Nazi Germans.

Little Panni and Big Panni were not afraid of the bombs. They feared for their lives from the Nazi persecutor. When they were eight and twelve years old they had to wear a yellow star, to tell the world that they were Jewish. The gentiles sneered and pointed their fingers at them. They wanted to kill all the Jews.

They had to move from their nice homes in Klotild utca to a ghetto house, where other Jews also were forced to live. The cruel soldiers came in and took many of their friends and relatives to concentration camps. Both their fathers had to go and work in labor brigades, where they cleared away the debris caused by the bombs. In these brigades they were barely given any food, only thin soup and bread, and their fathers became thin and developed coughs and aches.

The girls did not read anymore. They just sat and sat and prayed and hoped that the war would end and that they could go home again and live like little girls in other parts of the world, free of worry and anxiety about discrimination and torture.

Their wish came true in January 1945, when Budapest was liberated by the Russian military troops and they could go home again.

To Julia: When I Was Eight

My Dear Julia,

Today I want to tell you how my life was when I was your age.

When I was eight years old I lived in a big apartment house near the Danube River in Budapest, Hungary. We had to take an elevator to the fifth floor to our home. My family consisted of my mother, Nyunyu; my father, Apu; my sister, Panni; my grandparents, Nagypapa and Nagymama; our German governess, Fràulie; and our maid, Annus. The apartment opened into the entry hall, where people who came to visit could sit. One then came to the dining room, the living room, and the children's room, where my sister and I slept. There was a bedroom for my parents, a bedroom for my grandparents, bedrooms for the governess and the maid, the kitchen, pantry, and bathroom, and there was a separate toilet in the back.

My sister and I shared a bedroom, and outside of it we had a balcony, where we sometimes played. We played with our dolls, dressing them and talking to them as little mothers do. My doll's name was Zsuzsa and my sister's doll was Judy. There were two beds in our room and a low table, where we drew pictures, did our homework, and ate some of our meals. In the evening we ate in the dining room with the adults.

In those days there was no television. All we had was a radio, kept in the living room where the family would gather to listen to the news. It was wartime and we all wanted to hear what was happening in our country and with our neighbors, Austria, Yugoslavia, and Romania. My father was in charge of turning the dials, adjusting the volume, and we learned to be quiet while the announcer read the news report. It was important to us all.

My grandmother was sick in bed when I was eight. She had suffered a heart attack and had developed pneumonia. She had to use oxygen and was put into a tent made out of bed sheets. We could visit her in her room when she came out of the tent for a short while. My grandmother liked to knit and crochet. She taught me some of the patterns that she knew.

My grandfather traveled to the countryside on business and was away for many weeks at a time. He was a cattle buyer and he would go to farms and inspect cows and calves for shipment to larger livestock farms. My grandfather wore boots and riding pants and had a nice outdoor smell, probably from the hay and the cows in the barns, where he spent his time. He often brought back fruits and vegetables from the farms for us to share.

My dad worked in a bank. He smoked cigarettes and smelled of eau de cologne. My father wore suits and starched white shirts with a different necktie each day. He walked me to school when I was eight. His bank was near my school. He often said, "We must take big steps today because we are late." We did.

My mother—Nyunyu, as you knew her too, Julia—was a wonderful homemaker, an accomplished cook and hostess, and a very caring mother. She helped me with my homework, especially when I had to draw illustrations for my geography handbook. We had to show what products were made in different regions of Hungary. She helped me practice the piano. Nyunyu played piano as a young girl and she continued to practice as an adult. She read music and kept me in time with the rhythm of each musical piece. It was hard to practice every day. I got a star when I did well on my pieces.

My parents often had friends over and played bridge. Bridge is a card game for four people or for eight people playing two games. They spent many evenings drinking coffee, enjoying homemade pastries, and playing the card game they enjoyed. They laughed, talked, and had a good time then.

On Sundays we used to go on hikes and outings into the Buda hills. Sometimes we took walks on Margaret Island, which is a park-like island in the Danube. When it was summer we went swimming in one of the swimming pools of Budapest. We liked the Gellért baths best of all because there were artificial waves in that pool. Nobody swam in the Danube River because it was too cold and too deep. It think it was also polluted, even in those days. Remember, Julia, when I was eight years old, the year was 1940, a long time ago.

I look back happily on my childhood. Someday I hope to show you the city where I grew up.

With love,

Your Grandmother, Ági

A Wonderful, Awful Vacation

The sun was shining bright, the air was balmy, and the pool looked so enticing. The water was emerald blue, the sky cloudless, the palm trees gently waved their large green fronds in the breeze. The vacationers grabbed their large bath towels, secured a shady lounge chair and table near the waterfall at the pool, jumped into the water, then did ten laps in the kidney-shaped pool. So refreshing and invigorating! The vacationers felt revived, rejuvenated, and hungry. They walked down the well-groomed path, with bougainvilleas blooming in many shades of pink, and soon arrived at the ocean beach.

Yellow and green lounge chairs and large white umbrellas offered comfort and protection from the sun at its apex. Young attractive couples were snuggling close to each other. Mexican vendors brought tropical fruits, cut up into large plastic cups, and another vendor carried a cooler with freshly caught shrimp. There were parachutes taking off with parasailers, a colorful collage of activity. Our vacationers hailed a waiter who brought them frosty beers in well-chilled glass mugs. The ocean was gently rolling to shore, kids jumping and frolicking in the waves. Paradise must have been like this, they thought. Before they dozed off, a guitar player appeared and strummed the chords for a lively song, "Cucuruc Paloma," the famed young *muchacha* sang. They were enveloped in music and rhythm.

The next day the skies were gloomy. Storm clouds gathered. It rained in torrents. There was nobody at the pool. The water was too cold without the rays of the sun. The beach was deserted. Nobody liked to shiver with the chilly gusts of wind coming from the ocean. The vendors took shelter in their palapas and caught up on mending their fishing nets. Nobody offered a song to the vacationers. They were indoors in their rooms watching the news on CNN.

Maybe they would catch a plane to return home before the week was up. The vacationers counted their pesos and packed their suitcases.

Paradise had its flaws, and home seemed more comfortable after all.

Unleashed

"Cigarettes and whiskey and wild, wild women...." This once was a cry of young men who wanted to live it up. They were the three outlets for letting go, letting go of inhibitions, of the strict mores of self-control, prudent behavior, and moderation in the fifties: to smoke, to drink, to carouse.

I, on the other hand, had been brought up with many limits: a young lady must pull her skirt below her knees when she sits down; she sips tea from a cup with her pinky raised slightly; she dabs her lips with her handkerchief; she averts her eyes and does not make eye contact with strange men; she is never too loud when she speaks; and she always minds her manners. This was intimidating and became habitual. I had become a conformist.

Then I finished college and got a job in San Francisco. I packed my well-pressed clothes and sensibly heeled shoes and got on a Greyhound bus. It was a three-day trip from Rockford, Illinois, to San Francisco, California. There were three stopovers: in Nebraska, Colorado, and Nevada. By the time the bus rolled into Omaha, I had unbuttoned my blouse to mid-chest. It was warm and humid. By Colorado, I had stripped off my girdle and let go of my stockings. And in Nevada I put on sandals and sported sunglasses to ward off the rays of the midday sun. I had finished with dainty cheese sandwiches and now enjoyed hamburgers with fries, like the rest of the passengers on the bus. My seat mate was a Chicano mother with a little boy and a baby at her bosom. They were traveling back to her family who were farm workers in the Central Valley, returning from a visit to her brother in Chicago, who was seriously ill. I learned about

220

patience and endurance from Maria through her speaking with her children and her calming songs during the long journey.

"Pedro, look out the window and tell me what kind of tree you see?" "Are those cows out to pasture?" "Look at that red car coming down the road. Is it a Ford or a Chevy?" "How can you tell?" "Where is it from?" "You can tell from the license plate." "We will stop soon and you can have more water then." "Look, your baby sister just went to sleep. You should rest too...."

Behind us an older man hummed on his harmonica. "Jimmy cracked corn and I don't care...."

A new world opened to my eyes. People were all different and yet there was a common humanity among us. We all wanted to be connected, comfortable, and yet follow our own dreams. We hoped for success in our chosen careers, a family, and a comfortable shelter. We wanted to see the world, and it did not matter how proper we were as long as we didn't step on others' toes. You could be loud. You could remain quiet. As long as you stayed in your own space, there was room for all.

My job in San Francisco was with a market-research firm. We did political polls and called people across the western United States. The job was demanding and you had to produce results. We made many calls to find people willing to chat on the phone for a half hour. I became a star interviewer. I listened to the voices on the other end of the line. I paid attention to what young and old had to say. I loved my work. Before long I was the supervisor for our team. I could afford a nicer apartment now. I had my private bedroom and a view of the Bay. I adopted a cat and felt pretty happy about my newfound independence. My prissy manners were but a memory. I was unleashed from useless conventions. I lived by my own rules and they worked for my lifestyle.

A Day at the Spa

Angela rarely looked into the mirror. She applied her makeup quickly—dabbed on some pink rouge and covered her lips with lipstick in two strokes. Brushing her hair was routine and done efficiently, from right to left, to fluff up her wavy brown hair. She would not contemplate her image for long. She only took a furtive glance at the overall effect and she would be on her way, to whatever she had to do.

When she turned fifty her family celebrated at a big gathering. She loved the attention she received from her sons, nieces, and nephew. She got practical gifts this time: fine soaps, fragrant candles, flowers, and bath oils. The most unusual gift was a gift certificate for a spa facial. She never had one before and was a little apprehensive about how invasive it could be. They would exfoliate her skin, use strong astringents and maybe even harmful chemical products. She considered it a torturous experience, similar to a trip to the dentist, where you are at the mercy of the technician who works you over. Curiosity got the best of her, and with the summer doldrums and spare time on her hands, she made an appointment at the spa.

A well-appointed reception area awaited her, with beauty products on display, magazines in a rack, and comfortable seats available. Orchids were growing in elegant flowerpots. Soon her attendant appeared and ushered her into a dressing room. A large, fluffy robe enveloped her, and slippers were placed on her feet. The first ritual was a warm and herbally fragrant footbath, where she was asked to soak her tired feet. The attendant checked the water temperature and allowed her time to immerse her toes. There were four other women alongside. All were sitting on couches, wrapped in robes and chatting with each other. Angela wondered why people so young would need body-rejuvenating treatments? How could they afford the cost of it, just barely out of school?

Her musing was interrupted by her attendant wiping her well-soaked feet with a warm terry cloth towel. "Please come with me," she urged. In the private treatment room the lights were dimmed and pleasant music played, sounding like water rippling over rocks, a panpipe whispering soothing tunes. She calmed down and relaxed.

Maria, the spa technician, wrapped Angela's hair in a comfortable headband to keep the tresses out of her face, placed a pillow under her knees, and put a towel under her chin. Then she started a long series of creams that she applied on Angela's forehead, chin, and neck, all the way to her earlobes and around her temples. The ointments smelled of lavender, thyme, and honey. She applied these with upward strokes, then feathery massages. Sometimes she put pressure on certain spots, then she smoothed it away with light fingers.

After this came a cucumber-and-yogurt mask that was cool and refreshing. It felt nice, Angela thought, when she applied it. While the mask did its magic, Maria gave Angela a hand-and-foot massage. She stretched the fingers and circled Angela's palm with roundabout, warming motions. She enveloped Angela's feet with milky lotion and relaxed all the tensions in those distant limbs.

Angela felt as if she were in a warm cocoon, far from the cares of the world. She drifted into pleasant thoughts and felt she was in a distant, comfortable place. Soon it was time for the mask to come off. A warm, lemon-scented towel was placed on her neck, then slowly lifted up her face. With a sure hand, Maria wiped off the yogurt goop and washed it off with some lemon oil. A little more dabbing and patting on her face and

Angela was told that she was finished.

Rising slowly from the reclining bed, Angela felt that the weight of the world had lifted from her shoulders. She felt light. Her steps were bouncy. She walked on air.

She looked into the mirror on her way out. A rosy-cheeked, smiling face greeted her. It was the pleasant look that she saw only when she was away, by the ocean, on vacation. She saw a renewed self, with a glimmer of self confidence reflected from her eyes. A day spent in the lap of luxury.

On the Way Home

"Yiskadal, veyiskadash, Sh'mei Rabba...." May the memory of my dear mother be for blessing. She died last Friday and I miss her so. She was ninety, had lived a good life, but still, she left behind a void. Her apartment needs to be sorted out and packed up. Her furniture should be given to the émigrés. Her papers have to be filed and put in boxes. Her clothes need to be packed up.

How can I find the time and strength to do all this when they have me on the morning shift at St. Vincent's Hospital in the ER, where there's not one quiet moment? Ambulances keep bringing in injured automobile victims and the Bowery bums after a night of drinking. I keep running from patient to patient, from supply room to the chart room, a bandage, a suture, another infusion, a new oxygen tank.... I am always on the go. My feet are killing me and my mind is in a cloud. I am still grieving, yet I have no time to reflect. I am running like a rabbit.

Now I have a little time to reset, between Irving Place and the Brooklyn exit. Lots of people squeezed in here today. It is stuffy and humid. I must have missed the 4:35 train and this is the rush hour. I wonder what this young man has on his mind, across the aisle from me. He keeps fidgeting and is getting more nervous as he rocks back and forth. He must be on speed.... He keeps looking at me. I'll try to ignore it so he doesn't get crazy ideas in his head. Maybe I remind him of his mother or maybe he is not feeling well.

I am scared of this man. I have seen that crazy look in my manic patients' eyes before. This guy is up to no good. With

all these folks there is nowhere to go. The car is too crowded.
I wish I could leave, but I don't want to draw any attention to
myself. I'll just say another prayer and hope to make it out of
here unharmed.

Sh'ma Yisroel, please protect me from harm. Why me? Why
today when my heart is so heavy? Why, God?

He is on me!

He is hurting me now!

He is choking me!

I can't escape!

I can't breathe!

Oh God…!

A Life-Altering Decision

The three siblings called for a family gathering. They had to make a momentous decision in their father's health care: to operate again and put him through more discomfort in the slight glimmer of hope of eventual recovery, or to discontinue the life-support system that he was receiving. He had suffered for months, and their optimism for recovery had diminished. Two of the siblings were in favor of the second open-heart surgery, but the youngest felt that their dad had suffered enough and should be allowed to close his eyes forever.

Robert was a sportsman, a fit and athletic man of seventy, when the doctors diagnosed a rare cardiac condition, called pericarditis. The operation was performed in a local hospital to free his heart from the calcification that constricted it from pumping freely. Fluid backed into his lungs and caused edema. He could not breathe. He could not move about. He was out of breath after a few steps to the bathroom. He needed oxygen. He was bedridden. He had to be fed and all he was able to do was lie quietly, motionless in his room. He was not interested even in watching TV.

"What's the use?" he said. "Life is not worth living like this."

But his doctors were interested in his condition. They rarely saw a patient with pericarditis, so they experimented and tried different methods to help him to recover. They drained the fluid from his chest. They increased his oxygen intake. They prescribed a strong diuretic and another heart medication. Nothing seemed to work. He lapsed into depression. His weight dropped dramatically. Then a new surgeon offered to

227

repeat the cardiac surgery.

This was our moment in time, when the decision had to be made by his children to continue or to give up. The two siblings who wanted to pursue the medical options won out, over their sister, who wanted to spare her dad from suffering. It was a life-affirming decision and a reasonable one. He survived the second open-heart procedure, and a few weeks later started to breath without the help of oxygen.

Now the prognosis has improved. They hope to get him back on his feet shortly. If all goes well, he will make it to the golf course eventually.

Homeless

She fled to freedom across the Hungarian border because she could not live under Communist control. She wanted to go to college and become a medical researcher. In Hungary they would not let her be enrolled. She was a middle-class political undesirable. Her parents were not from the working classes. She had no chance for an education. So she packed a small backpack with a change of clothes and went to the border, where she joined a group of refugees who were crossing that night. They walked through minefields and dense forest and then along a busy highway until they reached Wien in the morning.

She got there exhausted, dirty, and bewildered. Where would she stay? Luckily she had an address that her best friend had given her at the last minute. "Trudie Gold," her friend had said, "will give you a clean bed for a couple nights. She was my nanny before the war. She lives close to the Westbahnhof, the train station. Call her."

She found a phone booth, gathered the shillings that her friend had given her, took a deep breath, and dialed the number. "Fraulein Gold?" But the phone just rang on and on. Again and again she tried. No answer.

Disappointed and exhausted, she took her place among the homeless on Europa Platz. It started to rain. She closed her eyes and wrapped her raincoat tighter, for warmth.

Dilemma

The Frank family lived in Wien, in the first district of a very pleasant residential section off the Kärntner Strasse. They had a five-room flat on the second floor, with a balcony. The Franks were merchants. They sold textiles and sewing supplies to the retail public. Papa Frank inherited his shop from his dad, Maurice, an honored and respected man about town. Papa Frank was forty-six years old now, a family man. He loved his wife, Anna, a vivacious and attractive homemaker. They had one son, Peter, age twelve.

Peter attended the gymnasium on the Graben until the Germans occupied Austria in 1941. They marched in and annexed Austria to Germany. They took over the government and systematically restricted the civil liberties of the Jews. Jews could no longer attend public schools. Jews could not hold any public office. Jews could not own property. Jews could no longer practice law or do anything freely. There were new rules and regulations weekly to make life miserable for all. So Peter could not attend the gymnasium, where he was an excellent student.

His parents enrolled him in the rabbinic seminary in the Jewish part of Wien, in the Judengasse. He went because he was motivated to learn and study both secular and religious studies. He got used to wearing a skullcap and a *talith*. His parents were reform Jews and thought that if they assimilated with the Christians they would blend in and be accepted as mainstream Austrians. They did not know that the Nazi regime would take over. Every night when Papa Frank came home from his store he was more worried about the safety of his family. He heard of labor camps and deportations in Poland and in other neighboring countries. He no longer believed that it could not happen in Austria. The Germans were ruthless and cruel, and the extermination of the Jews was the aim of the Third Reich. Hitler convinced the multitudes that it was the Jews that caused all their economic problems. Without Jews, prosperity and world domination would be achieved, a maniac's pipe dream.

Then one day a letter came from America. It was Anna's brother Andy, who wrote after a long silence. Andy was a small factory owner near Chicago. He had left Austria after the First World War after an anti-Semitic episode at the university. He was an American now, with a Protestant wife, and commanded respect as a well-to-do industrialist. Andy offered to adopt Peter and pay for his transit and later his education in the United States. Peter would have an opportunity to be free of persecution from the Germans. He could start a new life in Chicago. The Frank family had to make the decision right away so the visa could be processed. There was no time for delay.

Peter felt confused, in a terrible conflict about the choice he had to make: leave his parents behind in the grip of the Nazis for a life in America, or remain with his parents and share the uncertain future there. He spent sleepless nights and wandered aimlessly on the Ring and sat on park benches. Finally he went to the synagogue for guidance in his quandary.

"Should I go, or should I stay? Should I forgo everything that I have known and what matters to me the most, my parents and my home, to live in comfort and prosperity with strangers in a foreign land?"

One ending:

Then his eyes glanced at the Ten Commandments on the pulpit of the synagogue. "Honor thy father and mother that you should live long and fulfill this commandment." This was a message sent from the heavens to him. His life must be lived

231

with his parents no matter what fate awaited them. He must stay here and honor his duties as a son.

He felt lighter, and his eyes shined with a new zeal. His calling in his life was to be the son, the only son in the family, who could comfort his parents and carry on the family traditions. He would not forsake them as long as he lived. The Nazis would not diminish their family's bond of love and loyalty. He would continue to see his dad, as he slipped the key in the lock and entered the house smiling and warmly embracing his mother. They would sit at the dinner table together, light the *Shabbat* candles, and compliment his mother on how light the *matzah* balls were again. He would continue his Jewish studies and meet his friends on the street corner for a manly talk about the girls across the street. Maybe Annabel, the brunette, would smile at him.

Another ending:

Peter thought day and night about the American uncle's generous offer. He dreaded being separated from his parents but maybe it would not be for long. The war must end, hopefully soon, and they could be reunited again. In a few years he would be finished with school and he would get a job in his uncle's factory. He would save all his money and bring his parents to America. They would all start a new life there and they would be free of anti-Semitism and persecution. He could not miss this great opportunity. No matter how hard it seemed to be at the moment.

Csöpi*

(*means "tiny" in Hungarian)

Csöpi was a fluffy little poodle. He came into our lives after the war. Uncle Béla thought that his two nieces, Panni and Ági, needed a new toy to play with. But this was not as easy as he thought.

The Biró family lived on the fourth floor of an apartment building near the Danube in Budapest. Csöpi had to be transported down many flights of stairs to walk near the grassy strip by the tennis courts to get his exercise. Then up in the small elevator to the fourth floor. He objected to being on a leash.

The year was 1947. The war had ended in 1945 and life did not settle back into a routine for at least another year. Peasants brought food to the city on overcrowded trains. Vendors set up stalls near the boulevard and traded live chickens for men's shoes. Flour in sacks was now measured into pillowcases. Paper was a shortage item after the war. People brought their own bottles for milk to be ladled into.

The Biró family moved into this spacious apartment after the war. Their own home, also on the fourth floor but in a neighboring building, was in ruins after an allied bomb attack. Luckily, enough of the furniture could be salvaged to furnish this apartment. A big bookcase was put on coasters. The tables, armchairs, beds, and other furniture were carried by strong moving men with ropes as booster straps. The chandelier, carried carefully, was placed in the center of the living room.

The family lived in one room only for a while. Then Grandfather, Panni, and Ági slept in one room while the parents shivered in the unheated living room. The central heating had not started up yet. To be warm, the Birós used a small coal-stoked stove in the room facing the courtyard, next to the kitchen.

The two girls returned to school in 1946, and Apu, their dad, was once again busy at the bank. Life was still hard, and owning a dog was more of a challenge than a treat. The two girls rose to the occasion. Csöpi had his daily walk, occasional bath in the kitchen, and many food treats delivered to his doggie dish. He yelped happily and jumped for joy when the girls came home from school. Panni was eleven years old by then and Ági, a teenager.

Panni was in the Pioneer Youth Group as required by law. She wore a white blouse with a Pioneer scarf tied around her neck, with red, white, and green edging and a hammer-and-sickle logo in the middle of the cloth. This was under socialism and the government dictated people's activities. The Pioneers, fashioned after the Girl Scout movement, were to perform community services, such as helping indigent old people with food deliveries. They spent a lot of time learning socialist songs and marched in the parades. Panni was a good soldier. She appeared to be enjoying all the required activities.

Csöpi grew into a butterball. He explored the flat, got into tight spaces, and often had to be rescued because he could not free his now-rotund body. Then one day he chewed on the electric cord and almost got electrocuted. Luckily, Uncle Béla was visiting the Birós and he saved his life, but from this moment on, Csöpi's days in Budapest were numbered.

Mother Nyunyu exclaimed, "This dog does not belong in the city. This dog should be sent to the country where he can roam, explore, and be free."

Grandfather transported him to the vineyard in a big, airy food basket, with a stick of salami. The salami lasted until

Csöpi jumped to freedom in Badacsony hours later. The girls shed a few tears at the loss of their playmate but soon got back to their books and homework. Panni went off to her required Pioneer meeting and shared the story of Csöpi's departure with her best friend.

Maybe this summer, when their school was out, they would see a bigger and bouncier Csöpi as they visited him in the vineyard.

Anna

Her name was Anna Mária, but her nickname was always Panni. She was born in Budapest. After the war, while not yet in her teens, she came to America, where she was adopted by relatives, who changed her name to Ann.

Panni was a frail child and caught colds easily. Her governess tried to protect her from rain and wind. Panni responded angelically to such pampering and care, with smiles and clever sayings. When she didn't want her blonde hair washed she told Fräulie, *"Nicht waschen, nur nass machen."* "Don't wash it, only make it wet." Panni loved her dolls and would tuck them in gently for the night. When she was five, her uncle gave her a little poodle dog, named "Csöpi." She carried the dog around like it was a baby and covered it with her handkerchief so it would not get sunstroke. She would sneak bits of bread to it under the table when no one was looking.

This tender-hearted girl also had a serious temper. She would hold her breath until she turned blue. She had tantrums when things displeased her. She pounded the table and yelled at the top of her voice. Her older sister always gave in to her when she wanted a toy or a doll to play with. Panni was respected and even revered in the family. Nobody wanted to get on her wrong side.

Panni grew up to be a beautiful teenager. Her once thin blonde hair became lustrous and wavy. Her skin, once pale, became like ivory, with a slight peach-colored glow. Her lips were dainty and well curved. Her eyebrows formed a perfect arch over her warm, brown eyes. Boys followed her home from school. Teachers praised her for her diligent schoolwork. She got first prize in a speech contest, an honor that won her a free trip to Washington, D.C. She was seventeen then. Flying to the nation's capital to deliver her speech on freedom was a momentous event. She entered a midwestern college on a scholarship and decided to become a teacher. She loved little kids and felt that it would be a worthwhile goal to become a role model for youngsters.

She met a tall and handsome boy at a party. Roger was his name, a business major but a sportsman at heart. He wanted to become a golf pro not an accountant. The wedding was held after graduation at the local country club where Roger's parents were the managers. The golf course was Roger's backyard. The newlyweds spent their first year together on the pro circuit. They drove their old, well-worn Ford from one golf tournament to another. They shook hands with Bing Crosby, Arnold Palmer, and Lee Trevino. They clinked highball glasses with the best. But the monetary rewards, the prize money, never came their way. Roger was too tired after the cross-country drives to hit the ball below par. No one cheered his hole-in-one, because he would miss it by a stroke. Their savings ran out. Jobs had to be found. The whirlwind trips had to end.

Panni to the rescue! She got a teaching job with her well-earned credentials. The young couple settled into domestic bliss and bought a family house in the suburbs. The family grew to five, with three lovely children, two girls and a boy. And, of course, the family was not complete without a dog or two or three. The kids had to learn responsibility. Before long there were five dogs barking in the backyard. Each of the three kids had his or her own beloved puppy.

Panni became the head teacher and then the principal of a private grade school, the Growing Years Learning Center. The classrooms were filled with drawings of nature, displays, history maps. Each class had a pet—a turtle or snake or some hamsters.

Flower beds decorated the walks, and birds were fed in well-placed birdfeeders. A children's paradise! The enrollment grew and a new location was found to accommodate the bulging classrooms. New teachers were hired—a music specialist, an art instructor, and a sports monitor.

Dark clouds gathered on the blue skies. Panni started to have daily bouts with migraine headaches. The Tylenol no longer eased the cramps. Her colleagues told her to rest in the darkened room near the cafeteria after lunch. Still the pain got worse. Her eyes blurred as she read to the class. She could not carry on with her duties. She had to take a leave of absence from her teaching job and get medical help for her problem.

Her doctor diagnosed her symptoms to be "stress related." She had to get away. She needed rest with no clocks to watch, no high heels to wear, and no lesson plans.

Panni, Roger, the kids, and the dogs found a beach house down the coast, near the Mexican border. It was just big enough that they could be comfortable. It was less expensive to own and easier to manage. Panni's headache seemed to lessen day by day. She felt at peace in her new setting. No more rush.

She kicked off her shoes and reclined in her easy chair. She could smell the roses blooming nearby. She looked up at the cloudless sky and saw a bluebird landing on a branch nearby. She felt bliss and harmony at last.

Another Easter Celebration

We have a yearly tradition, to go to Annabella's house for Easter dinner. This was the tenth time that we were to partake in that special gathering around her dining room table.

I started getting ready early in the afternoon. I was bringing the appetizers and could not arrive late. I mixed the cream cheese, chopped the green onions, stirred in the sour cream, mustard, anchovy paste, and the paprika, for the spread; chilled the prawns in ice water before I put them around the cocktail sauce; and carefully wrapped the flowers in cellophane so they wouldn't crush. Then I picked my newest blouse, to wear with the blue cloisonné beads my cousin just sent me, and put on new shoes with matching tan stockings. I wanted to show that I cared enough to look my best for this occasion.

When we pulled up at Annabella's hillside residence, the door was open and the gate unlatched. We rang the bell, no answer. We walked in, nobody home. We were surprised and speechless. Had we come too early? Checking our watches, we confirmed that we were actually a half hour later than the invitation called for. Where could she be? In the garage? In the shower? No. Within minutes the other guests arrived. First Cindy, Annabella's cousin, with husband George in tow. They were loaded down with spring flowers, bottles of wine, and a large salad bowl with mixed greens visible under the Saran wrap. After them came Margaret and her mother, Mrs. Jones, walking slowly and leaning on her cane. They brought a pan with long-stemmed green asparagus, French bread in long loaves, and some boxes of Easter candy.

Since we were all such good friends, we invited them in and made them comfortable. George opened a bottle of wine and I put out my appetizers. In a few minutes some more people arrived, all laden with goodies. Then Cindy found a note taped to the refrigerator. It was Annabella's handwriting: "Back in ten minutes. Went to pick up the cake." The question was, how long ago did she leave?

After we toasted with our first glasses of wine, Annabella's car pulled up with our hostess in a frazzle: her hair was blowing in the wind, she was out of breath, and she was carefully balancing the cake box. In her hurry she had forgotten to close the car door.

"I could not find a parking spot near the bakery and I was circling around for half an hour. Then the cake was not ready. I had to wait for the inscription. I am a wreck and I didn't even start dinner before I left."

We looked at each other and made an unspoken plan. We had to give a hand to our hostess and get the festive meal together. She was too stressed to do it herself. Cindy put the roast in the oven. Margaret started the rice. I sliced the French bread and passed the appetizers around. George took the role of the bartender. My hubby put the chairs around the table and poured ice water in the glasses.

We chatted. We showed old Easter photos, shared baby pictures, told travel stories, then opened another bottle of wine and finished all the prawns. Cindy steamed the asparagus. Margaret tossed the salad. Two and a half hours flew by and everybody was having a good time. Then we heard the oven timer go off— the lamb roast was done to medium rare. George took out his carving knife and did his professional slicing job. Annabella opened the mint jelly and placed it on the festive Easter table. We were ready to sit down and say our prayers.

Thank God, and thank you, dear Annabella, for having us share another happy Easter together.

The lamb was fresh, and the food all consumed. Best ever was the dessert, a creamy, custard-like raspberry-whip cake with chocolate flowers and the inscription: "Friends together make the world go round," the motto of the day.

Dining at the Boca Roti

My two friends and I decided to dine at the West Portal Boca Roti restaurant. They advertise spit-roasted chicken as their special. When we arrived a hostess greeted us cheerfully.

"Do you wish to sit in the front, where you can see the street-cars turning, or in the back, where it is a little more quiet and private?"

We chose a booth in the rear. A crisp, white tablecloth and a bouquet of tiger lilies welcomed us to our table. The waitress lit two votive candles and we looked at our menus in their warm glow. The waitstaff brought soft and moist *focaccia* bread strips, along with a selection of ripe and green olives and virgin olive oil to dip our bread in.

The wine menu offered local as well as international selections. We chose a bottle of Zinfandel from the Sonoma Valley. Our group decided to try different entrées and share some appetizers. The antipasto tray had thin-sliced prosciutto ham, pickled porcini mushrooms, some chunks of provolone, white cheese, and some crunchy crudités—red bell peppers and carrot sticks. The second platter of delicacies included pickled squid, sliced red onions, and capers—a taste delight in its tart and pungent flavoring.

Soon our entrées arrived: half chickens redolent with rose-mary and new red potatoes, pan-roasted to a crisp; and thick, juicy pork chops accompanied by sautéed Swiss chard and yellow saffron rice. André was just cutting into his chicken leg when suddenly, the wine glasses shifted on the table. It felt as if they were on a boat and the ship's balance tilted sideways. After

242

the first jolt, a bigger and stronger upheaval followed. André looked around.

"It's an earthquake. Oh my God."

In a second the group took shelter under the strong wooden table. Glasses flew, the picture on the wall crashed to the floor, the restaurant became a chaotic scene with people screaming, some trying to get out of the confinement of the booths and away from the smoke that enveloped the kitchen area and now permeated the dining room. Then the plate glass window blew out, almost exploded, and shattered all over the entry way. People in its way could not escape the shards of glass. They were bleeding and calling for help.

The earthquake subsided. Silence. Then sirens began wailing and fire engines could be heard, lights flashing in the now-darkened street. Water from the sprinkler system flooded the kitchen, then flooded the restaurant with debris. Injured, bleeding, and hysterical patrons were tended to and comforted by friends. The once clean and crisp tablecloths were torn into bandage strips. The ice water still in some of the drinking glasses served to wash wounds. The delicious meals were delicious no longer, and everyone tried to pull themselves together, to get home, to determine the havoc there, and to start cleaning up.

Laughter Echoes....

The home I left behind
still brings tears to my eyes.
Why? I ask.
It's long in the past.
I am a grown woman now.
My hair is no longer brown.
I have a new home now,
a family that has grown.
New roots have formed
in a happy and free land.
Yet, I still long for Klotild utca
and its views to the River Danube,
those happy halls,
the kitchen where we used to talk,
gathering nightly. After all,
this bit of heaven brings my family back:
Apu glued to the radio,
Nyunyu chatting on the telephone.
My grandfather praying,
my sister and I playing with our dolls.
Cool breezes ruffle the window curtains.
The bread rises on the stove.
Laughter echoes through the halls.

Doctor

When the doctor is downcast
I, the patient, am worried.
Why, dear Doctor Z., did you not smile
as you came in to greet me.
Your expression was unusually wry.
You did say, "Hello, Agnes,"
but you forgot to add, "and how is your sister?"
It was only business today,
of Pap smears, and bilateral X-ray.
You probed around and tried to measure my cervix
and other areas of service to my treasured visit.
Please resume your smile
and give me once again a fine spiced friendship
along with the old medicine.

A Letter to My Youngest, Raul

My Dearest Son:
Burn the candles slowly
Where are you now?
How are you feeling? What are you thinking of?
Those faraway places?
Do you think of music?
Are chords and harmonics running through your head?
    Arpeggios and scherzos,
and pizzicatos moving fast?
Or are you worried
about paying the rent, feeding the cats, and protecting the new
    sofa
from the sharp claws of your animals?
Are your feet cold and wet
as you slosh through puddles coming home late at night
on dark, deserted paths?
It's been a long day, I know.
New York is noisy and crowded. People push and shove,
    pining for a quiet corner.
They wish only to look at their own front pages.
You will be home soon.
The table will be set, the wine glasses put out, with the soup
fast simmering on the stove.
You can start your day now
and live your private life. Burn the candles slowly.
You still have lots of time.

Two People in One Cocoon

The two of you are wrapped into one,
a mixed burrito of smile and frown.
Long brown hair and stubbly beard,
embraced, firmly entwined
into each other
and yourselves.
Is there a world outside?
Drink in each other's fragrance now.
Your happiness is tantamount.
The rest of the world does not count.

Marina

Marina, my very special niece! We love her dearly!
When she was born she brought sunshine.
The smile on her face is here today.
As a baby, she hardly ever cried.
As a youngster, she got along with her playmates.
As a student, she helped her mother correct papers.
(Her mother, my sister, ran a school those days named The
    Growing Years.)
Marina was a fine, diligent student,
a beauty queen when a teenager.
Then onward to college at Cal Poly, joining the sorority of
    her mother and mine, Gamma Phi Beta, to become a
    popular Greek (not geek).
She spent her junior year abroad in England,
graduating with flying colors in horticulture.
She traveled in Europe, then and later,
visiting family, with family including me and her mother,
    with highlights in Lugano, Florence, Paris, and—of
    course—Budapest, ever upbeat and tireless.
After college she moved to San Francisco where she became
    our closest family.
And she worked, very successfully, eventually returning to her
    field, horticulture.
But (alas for us) she returned to her immediate family in
    Southern California
to take over and mold into her own business, MIXED
    GREENS.

MARINA!
The smartest of businesswomen,
the most caring of nieces, the best homemaker,
the most creative party-giver!!!!
Her home is her castle and the prince in her life is her
    husband Jason!
(How not to mention her love of pets: her long-lived, happy
    Chester,
Pánchur, and Roger the dog and many others whose
    boundless energy brought happiness.)
Marina has packed a lot of fun into her young years. We salute
    her on turning 40!
Long live Marina. God bless you dearest!

Thoughts on My Friend's Death
August 11, 1999

I feel like shouting from the rooftops.
Only heaven can hear me now.
I need help to decide: why, why, why?
Gerti, why did you do it?
You were wise and knowing.
You were helping and guiding.
Friends, mothers, came to you in need of advice.
Children who could not find their path sat at your desk.
How could you have enough of living,
of laughing, or even crying,
and of looking at the sky.
The sky was your friend.
It helped you fall asleep at night.
Looking from your bed to the starry display
and the changing patterns of the clouds
and moon.
You wondered about its dramatic displays.
You welcomed the light of the dawn after stormy nights.
Your pine tree in the window grew as the years passed
from seedling to a silver-tipped giant that reached up to the
     second story.
It spread its branches across the house.
Your dining table was always set with delicate china and fine
     linens.
The table was laden with fragrant dishes:
lecso paprika, tomatoes with sharp sausages.

It tickled the palate.
The guest was seated so that the pine tree was in their view,
beauty to behold,
while your chair faced the white-washed wall.
The conversation at the table was thoughtful and
    introspective.
You listened and advised your friends,
"What seems to be on your mind?"
"What is your worry?"
"Is your son distancing himself from you?"
"Does he act like a stranger now?"
"Well, his job is too demanding and that occupies his mind.
He is still leaning on his parents for support because at work
    he has to stand tall and unbending.
Allow him to lean on you for a while longer."
You understood us all but we never knew you, Gerti.
Your thoughts were private and solitary.
You left us too soon.

In Memoriam: Sam Wellborn

A life well lived
is
well remembered.
The need to reflect with sadness
to recall little stories and personal memories
and tell them to others,
completes the picture for those who knew the man.
To share the treasures buried but not forgotten.
He stood up and defended.
He listened and cared.
He was a friend to his daughters and all who came.
He made his wife laugh often.
He knew facts.
He cooked.
He tended orchids.
He created rhythms and blues in the classroom
... always celebrating and renewing the spirit of young and old.

Palm Spring

(To be again)
in Palm Springs
in the evening
with breezes
gently
blowing
embracing
caressing
bougainvillea petals
floating down
dropping on the terrazzo floor
covering the ground
randomly, carelessly.
Heaven cannot be more welcoming
than
Palm Springs in the spring.

A Toast

To all the lives we gently touched
in the desert
and
near the sea!
First to Dean
who is dapper
and
elegant
at sixty or more.
He cuts a dashing figure and talks a good talk.
He knows the desert where he raises colorful flowers and
shades them daily from sand and sun.
Then to Andrea and Bill
as they look after their young ones
surround them with toys and intricate games
keep them occupied and busy at play.
Marina and now her beau Jason
two hip ones
who keep romantically engaged
while
they work and manage
employees at bay
and their households
as well as canine strays.
Then our dear ones Panni and Roger
who live on their well run estate
where crystal glistens and silver is polished.

A JOURNEY

It's always elegant
the house where they stay.
God bless them all,
'til we get together again.

Moving

Thank God for routine,
even more for sanity.
For, when chaos surrounds,
where would my spirit be:
packing and schlepping
upstairs and down,
lifting and sitting
through old pillows of down.
Decades of collecting
belongings galore.
Lets give it to Goodwill,
Glide Church or just throw it out.
There go the memories,
treasures of old.
A fresh life is starting,
and we must clean up our new
HOME.

Letter from Apu to Panni and Roger, dated October 31, 1963
(translated on opposite page)

[October 31, 1963]

The stamps on the envelope are for Sylvia.

My Sweet Little Panni and Roger,

Your letter full of concern and worry touched me deeply. Instead of my writing to you, Klára answered your letter because I was unable to write then. Unfortunately, once again I suffered a serious illness. I had pneumonia three times consecutively which responded only to the newest, most effective English-made antibiotic. For four days I was injected every six hours, day and night. After all this I suffered a second heart attack. When my fever went down they allowed me to come home which I welcomed because I was afraid of a fourth relapse of pneumonia which I may not survive. I am very weak and spend most of the time in bed. I lost 17 kg. [35 lb.]. You can imagine how bad I look. I am under constant doctors' care. Klára spends most of the day here, nursing me. Ilonka is here all day too. I am recovering slowly in spite of the wonderful care I receive. I am afraid I will no longer be able to return to my job. Not getting my salary will greatly affect how I can cover my monthly expenses. We will wait and see how things work out.

I was happy to read in your letter that you are enjoying this school year. I think I know that you like to teach first graders. Twenty-five kids in the classroom is really manageable but it is still a serious task to teach them all to read and write.

Ági wrote me about Roger's new job. He is working—as I understand—for a family-owned insurance company. They must be stingy— here employees get twelve days vacation in the first year of employment.

Do you remember that today is a sad anniversary. Today makes fourteen years since you two left home. I recall every detail of that day, as if it happened today.

If you have time, write sometime. I hug you and embrace you with love,

Apu

Postcard from Apu to Panni and Roger, dated September 12, 1961
(translated on opposite page)

A JOURNEY

[September 12, 1960]

[From the cardiac rehab hospital in Balatonfured]

My Dearest Little Panni and Roger,

Your two postcards, written on your trip, arrived in Budapest the day of my departure on Sept. 9. My sister Klára sent it to me here. I was very happy to have news from you so soon.

The airplane [you took] is very impressive. It traveled 4,000 kilometer distance in three hours. I hope you were able to rest on your vacation and you were able to start your teaching assignment with renewed strength. I imagine how happy all the relatives and friends [in Illinois] were to see you both. Andy, it appears, has chronic hay fever but that is an easy to handle illness. Grandmother Sorensen is a strong person. I am happy that she is well. I hope that Roger's parents are well too.

My [cardiac] examination is scheduled for today and tomorrow. After that I start my medication regimen. Otherwise I am feeling all right. One of my old roommates shares my room again, the third member didn't make it. The poor fellow died a few weeks ago.

I am planning to spend my vacation doing business errands for Klára. She got the visa [to see her nephews in London] and plans to leave early next month. She wrote down your address. She will write to you when she is away.

My little sweetheart, write to me at this address while I am here. I embrace you with hugs and send many kisses.

Apu

Postcard from Apu to Panni and Roger, dated June 3, 1961 (translated on opposite page)

A JOURNEY

[June 3, 1961]

Dearest Little Panni and Roger,

*I got news from Ági. She was very sad that you could not spend the
Memorial Day weekend together.*

*The much awaited summer vacation will soon be here. You much
deserve the rest and relaxation.*

*My dearest Roger, your birthday is also approaching [June 11]. Please
accept my heartfelt good wishes for this occasion. May God grant you
many more birthdays in good health and happiness.*

*Dearest little heart, now that your summer vacation starts I am
hoping that you will have more time to write to me. You know how
eagerly I wait for your letters.*

Wishing you both the very best, hugs and kisses.

From your Apu

The Biró-Hochstadter family, 1900

Gyuri and Józsi Oblath, and their nanny

Józsi and Clara Oblath, c. 1914

Ignácz Szlovák

Móricz and Aranka
Szlovák, 1920s

Móricz and Aranka in
the Tatra Mountains,
c. 1920

Sári Biró, around age 18

Zoltán and Nyunyu's first apartment, Budapest, 1925

Dining room cabinet, Zoltán and Nyunyu's first apartment

Nyunyu in the master bedroom

Zoltán and Nyunyu in their living room

Laci Oblath, Ági and Sári Biró, 1935

Ági, Nyunyu, and Baby Panni

Ági and Panni,
1938

Ági and Panni,
Badacsony, 1940

Ági, Panni, and Ági Méhes, 1945

Biró family, post-prison

Panni, Nyunyu, and Ági, 1949

Laci, Móricz, Nyunyu, Panni, and Badacsony village friend, 1940

Agnes and Shike, wedding couple, at the Edgewater Hotel, 1954

32 Taraval, our first home in San Francisco, California, 1964

Dan, 1960

Dan's second birthday, at Homewood Terrace

Andre, Agnes,
and Dan, 1964

Agnes and the boys,
1965

The Rothblatts at home, at 32 Taraval

Shike, Raul, Andre, and Dan at Searsville Lake, 1968

Andre's school photo, 1965

Andre, Stefan, Andrea, and Roger
Rubendall

The boys, 1968

Dan's bedroom door

Andre in Venice

Raul's high school graduation, 1982

Raul and his cello, c. 1983

Andre, Dan, Raul, and Nyunyu

Andre, Dan, and Nyunyu at 32 Taraval

Clara Rothblatt (Shike's mother), Agnes, David
and Renee Rothblatt, and Naomi Rothblatt

Elza Slovak's family in Romania, with daughter Julia and son-in-law
Lajos Farkas

Agnes and Shike on his first visit to Hungary

Shike with moustache

The Oblaths in London: Laci, Gyuri, Susan, and Gerda, 1982

Sylvia Slovak, Panni, Andy Slovak, and Roger Rubendall, Tucson, 1980s

Nyunyu, 1983

Panni, Agnes, and Nyunyu, 1990

Agnes and Nyunyu at Nyunyu's ninetieth birthday

Nyunyu and Panni, 1994

Nyunyu's grave, Colma, California

Szlovák grave, Budapest

Apu Zoltán's grave,
Budapest

Rothblatt clan, with cousin Leni Morris

Shike, Agnes, Dan, and Jayne

Roger, Marina, and Panni, 1999

Julia *(far right)* at thirteen, receiving first prize in an L.A. art
competition

Agnes and Shike, 1999

Anita at Cheryl's wedding

Cheryl and Gary Lerner,
Brooklyn, 2008

Anna Win and Stefan Rubendall, engaged, 1999

Lauren and Christopher
(Andrea's kids)

Lauren and Madeline (Stefan's
daughter)

Standing: Murray Kapell, unidentified
relative, Brian, *Seated:* Shike, Alec Lerner

Jayne, Julia, and Agnes in Budapest, 2002

Julia, 2010

Julia, 2006

Raul and Jennifer, 2006

Charlotte, Jennifer, and Raul at Jennifer's grandmother, Omi's, ninetieth birthday, 2010

Above: Rubendall memory book cover, with Andrea and Marina in Budapest.
Opposite page: memory book page

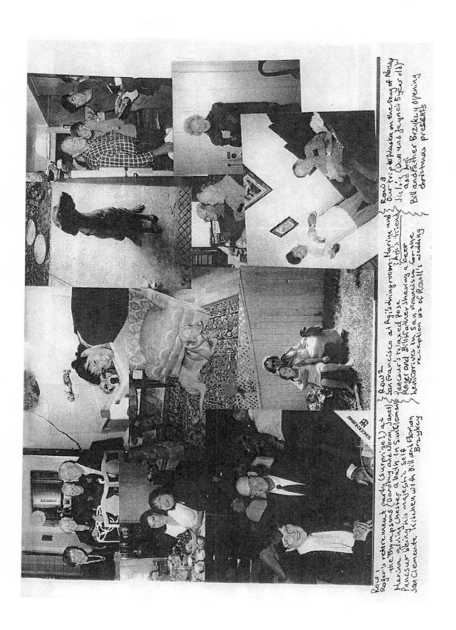

Row 1
Roger's retirement party (surprise!) at
the Thompsons (Dorothy and John Janet)
Marina giving Chester a bath in SunClemente
Pancsur being his majestic self
SanClemente Kitchen with Bill and Florian
Braysky

Row 2
SanFrancisco at Ag's living room Marina and
Pancsur's relaxed Pose
Roger and Bill (father) sharing a beer
he'd arrives in SanFrancisco for the
reception the of Roall's wedding

Row 3
Our trip to Alaska on the Ferry at Norway
Julie, (Dan and Jayne's 5 year old)
and Ag
Bill and father Braysky opening
christmas presents

297

The family, 1999

Agnes and Shike, Alaska cruise, 2003

CPSIA information can be obtained at www.ICGtesting.com
Printed in the USA
LVOW100412310312

275578LV00002B/36/P